MANUAL FOR SOUTHERN REGIONS

Committee on the Preparation of a *Manual for Southern Regions*

L. M. Brooks, Chairman, *University of North Carolina*
H. C. Brearley, *Clemson College*
Katharine Jocher, *University of North Carolina*
E. W. Knight, *University of North Carolina*
E. T. Krueger, *Vanderbilt University*
H. E. Moore, *University of North Carolina*

Under the authorization of

THE INSTITUTE ON SOUTHERN REGIONAL DEVELOPMENT
AND THE SOCIAL SCIENCES

held at Chapel Hill, North Carolina

June 17-27, 1936

The Six Major Regions Basic to the Southern Regional Study

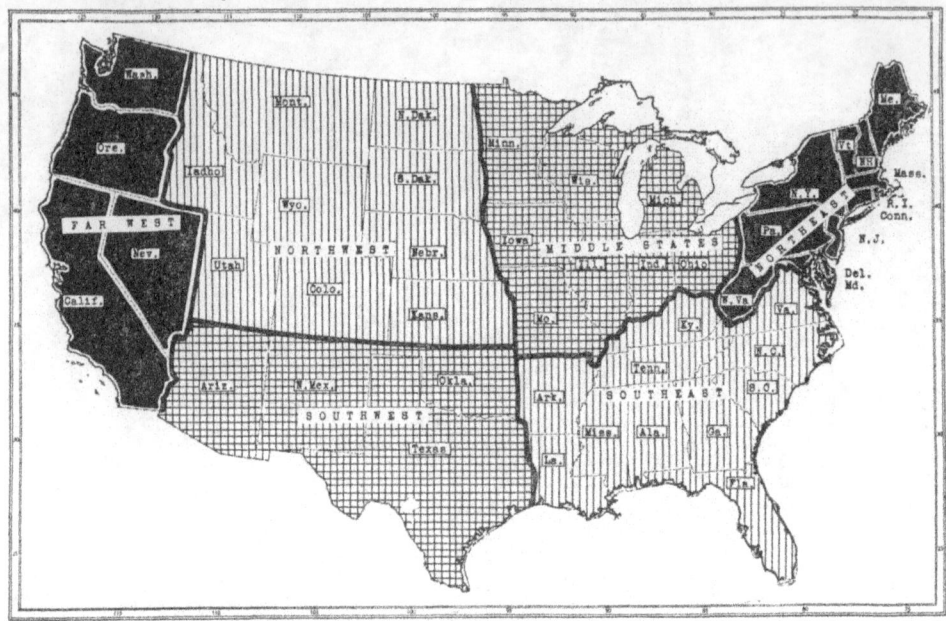

ABOVE: The sixfold regional division of the nation by states, utilized in statistical analysis of the southern regional study, state lines being essential for the use of census materials.

BELOW: The second map illustrates the same general sixfold division *if state lines could be ignored*. Thus the eastern bounds of the proposed shelter forest belt would mark the western bounds of the Middle States and the Southeast, properly including parts of North Dakota, South Dakota, Nebraska, Kansas in the Middle States, and parts of Oklahoma and Texas in the Southeast. So, too, parts of Ohio and Virginia would be included in the Northeast while the lower parts of Missouri and West Virginia would fall within the Southeast, as would a part of Indiana and Illinois. This is of course only approximate for illustrative purposes. For other similar maps and discussions, see Chapters III and X.

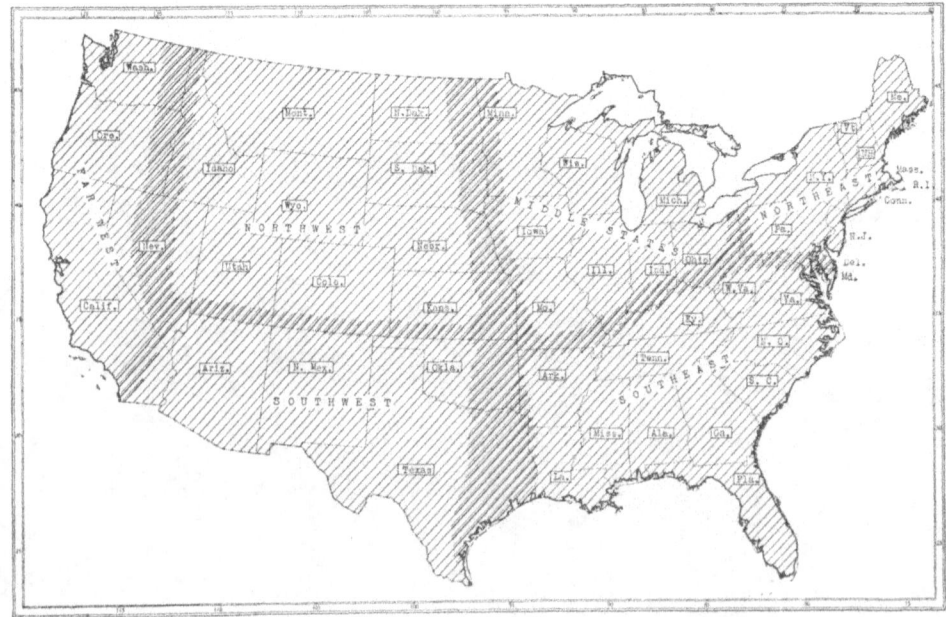

Reprinted from page 6 in *Southern Regions*.

Manual for SOUTHERN REGIONS

to accompany

SOUTHERN REGIONS OF THE UNITED STATES

by Howard W. Odum

By
LEE M. BROOKS
University of North Carolina

IN COLLABORATION WITH

WAYLAND J. HAYES, *Vanderbilt University*
HARRY E. MOORE, *University of North Carolina*
JENNINGS J. RHYNE, *University of Oklahoma*

CHAPEL HILL
THE UNIVERSITY OF NORTH CAROLINA PRESS
1937

COPYRIGHT, 1937, BY
THE UNIVERSITY OF NORTH CAROLINA PRESS

The Baker and Taylor Company, New York; Oxford University Press, London; Maruzen-Kabushiki-Kaisha, Tokyo; Edward Evans & Sons, Ltd., Shanghai; D. B. Centen's Wetenschappelijke Boekhandel, Amsterdam

THE UNIVERSITY OF NORTH CAROLINA PRESS
CHAPEL HILL, N. C.

ACKNOWLEDGMENTS

To Howard W. Odum for making possible this pleasurable work-venture based upon his comprehensive book to which this *Manual* is but a pointer, and for his ever patient helpfulness.

To the Committee appointed by the Institute on Southern Regional Development and the Social Sciences in June, 1936, for their guidance in the early stages and for their constructive criticisms as the work neared completion.

To the collaborators for their prompt and careful coöperation in preparing the substance of Units VI-XVII and XX-XXIII, and for their generous assistance in aiming to make the *Manual* as a whole of the utmost value to student and teacher.

To Katharine Jocher and the Institute for Research in Social Science at Chapel Hill, North Carolina, for detailed advice and technical assistance; to Mrs. S. P. Williams for her skill in typing the manuscript; and to Evelyn C. Brooks for valuable criticism at many points.

One further acknowledgment will be understood by those who have examined *Southern Regions of the United States*. From such a wealth of illustrative devices—six hundred maps, charts, and tables—it was extremely difficult to decide upon the plates to be reproduced in the *Manual*. The few illustrations taken from the original volume are but samples of what appears on its even-numbered pages.

Lee M. Brooks.

Chapel Hill, North Carolina
May, 1937

FOREWORD

RECENT DEVELOPMENTS in the United States have emphasized the significance of great American regions in relation to the progress of the nation and the total national culture. It is the purpose of this study program to present one approach to interpretation and direction in regional study and planning.

The *Manual* is, therefore, an accompaniment, an aid to the study of *Southern Regions of the United States* by Howard W. Odum. His work is a descriptive and analytic treatment of the older southeastern and the emerging southwestern regions of the United States, with emphasis upon planning for the increase of efficiency by utilizing the human power and natural resources with which the regions abound. The book, published by the University of North Carolina Press in 1936, contains 664 pages and approximately six hundred illustrative maps and charts. Comparisons within the southern regions and with the other four regions of the country are made possible by employing more than seven hundred indices or "culture items" of measurement. A few of the maps and charts are reproduced in this *Manual*, mainly to indicate the type of illustrative material in the book itself which will be referred to hereafter as *Southern Regions*.

The welfare of the nation is the welfare of states and regions. One part of the whole cannot be satisfactorily studied separately from the other parts. A glance at *Southern Regions* will reveal the national scope of the book. The roots and branches of this program of study will extend far beyond the fences of any region. Arguments for state or sectional sufficiency will find no support here. On the contrary, the fruitage of southern regional-national study should be profitable for the other four regions, especially in terms of thoughtful leadership. Such study, based upon research that cuts deep into the vitals of sore problems and that points with promise to better things, should be informative and stimulating for those who would think and work for a better balanced nation.

As for the two southern regions commonly referred to as "The South," they should be among "the very lovely lands of the world." Many a loyal southerner may well repeat inquiringly: "Should be?" And then the questions will accumulate, beginning with "Why not?" The study here projected would miss the mark if it did not answer some of the questionings, if it did not indicate prospects and promising possibilities.

Is the South awakening today and facing frankly the lights and shadows of the picture drawn by impressive fact? More than fifty years ago Sidney Lanier wrote these lines: "A vital revolution in the farming economy of the South, if it is actually occurring, is necessarily carrying with it all future southern politics, and southern relations, and southern art, and such an agricultural change is the one substantial fact upon which any really New South can be predicated."[1] Against the glamorous past even contemporary orators, novelists, and a few of the more statesmanlike politicians have begun to see the great southern portion of the country scarred and threatened by the wastage of land and man power.

King Cotton has toppled from his throne as the exclusive-crop tyrant in the Southeast. "The ancient order of cotton culture in the Old South is doomed," says a powerful little book entitled *The Collapse of Cotton Tenancy*. "Sweeping changes in southern farming must come swiftly if millions of former plantation workers are not to be completely wrecked— if the region itself is not to suffer violent ruin." Cotton is not alone as it totters toward collapse; other ideas and practices are being dethroned by hard fact and circumstance, for the very soil of the South is washing away largely because of land abuses due to negligence and enslavement to undesigned economy.

As planless crop habits wane, dilemmas insistently rise up. Shall the South and the country as a whole move by design or by drift? Can any region plan its way alone? Will any of the substantial values of our democracy be sacrificed if an effort is made to plan our way rather than just to muddle along? What will happen to our vaunted civilization if some social engineering is not done? Can we do no better than to say "hands-off," "let things take their course"? Glance at pages 217 and 599 of the book and "think on these things." If regional pride and American democracy are as fine, as worth saving as we think they are, we shall probably have to pride ourselves less and prod ourselves more in facing old questions and new challenges in terms of courageous and patient action. It is being said of modern civilization that it must either plan or perish. Is this not also true of the nation and the region?

What is the foundation question for the South? It is this: Can the Southeast and the Southwest with all their resources yet remaining to be restored and used, continue to be satisfied with numerous forms of deficiency and with narrow margins of existence such as poor food, bad housing, short schooling, demagoguery unparalleled, tolerance of intolerance, and all that

---

[1] Quoted from the *Progressive Farmer*, January, 1937, p. 58.

which spells drift instead of thrift? This is the substance of the big question that recurs throughout the book.

Fraught with vast meaning is "the dramatic struggle of a large and powerful segment of the American people for mastery over an environment capable of producing a superior civilization, yet so conditioned by complexity of culture and cumulative handicaps as to make the nature of future development problematical." Two pictures then: power, ability, and favorable environment on the one hand; cross-currents, cross-purposes, racial prejudice, religious narrowness, and piled-up handicaps of many kinds on the other hand—the whole picture, when set in the stereoscope of the future, blurred with doubt and with no clear delineation of what is to be.

It is a task of high patriotism to be willing to face facts realistically with courage and with purpose, to translate studied knowledge into well-tempered action, to grapple with complexities that show little inclination to become simpler, to help set in motion currents of new thought and life for the sake of the region and the nation.

It is with some of the more prominent "complexities of culture and cumulative handicaps" that we shall deal in this *Manual*. Only by examining conditions as they are will the studious mind be able to see ahead for the South and the nation. Knowledge comes first, then coöperative action unhindered by emotionalism, individualism, or sectionalism. Coöperation there must be from within and from without the region.

Thoughtful people—especially students, teachers, preachers, social workers, citizens, laborers, clerks, club leaders, politicians, industrialists, farmers, lawyers, doctors, housewives, young and old, rich and poor—will realize that the plight of the South is no mere academic problem. It is not a one-region problem. "It is stark reality. The Southern States, like the nation, are in the remaking; they have their big chance. How long will the option last? The South has reflected a peculiar fortune and social heritage often likened unto Germany in the sense that facing a crisis it has a tendency to take the wrong road." If these words from page 217 seem rather strong, test them out objectively and specifically. Vigorous thinking and resolute action were never more needed than now.

CONTENTS

	PAGE
ACKNOWLEDGMENTS	vii
FOREWORD	ix
INTRODUCTION TO PROGRAM OF STUDY	I

The Land

UNIT		PAGE
I.	THE OBJECTIVES OF THE SOUTHERN REGIONAL STUDY	9
II.	GEOGRAPHIC FACTORS AND PHYSICAL SETTING	19
III.	CULTURAL EQUIPMENT AND HISTORICAL BACKGROUNDS	27
IV.	EMERGING CULTURE PROBLEMS AND SITUATIONS	35
V.	BASIC FACTORS OF REGIONAL EXCELLENCE AND A NEW REGIONAL ANALYSIS	43
VI.	REGIONS OF NATURAL RICHNESS AND ABUNDANCE (ORGANIC)	51
VII.	REGIONS OF NATURAL RICHNESS AND ABUNDANCE (INORGANIC)	59
VIII.	REGIONAL TECHNOLOGY, DEFICIENCY AND WASTE (LAND)	67
IX.	REGIONAL TECHNOLOGY, DEFICIENCY AND WASTE (MAN)	75
X.	AN AGRARIAN COUNTRY	81
XI.	MEASURES OF INDUSTRY AND WEALTH	87
XII.	MEASURES OF INDUSTRY AND WEALTH (CONTINUED)	95

The People

XIII.	THE SOUTHERN PEOPLE	99
XIV.	THE EDUCATION OF THE PEOPLE	107
XV.	THE EDUCATION OF THE PEOPLE (CONTINUED)	115
XVI.	POLITICAL GENIUS AND GOVERNMENT FINANCE	121
XVII.	PUBLIC AND PRIVATE SOCIAL SERVICES	129
XVIII.	RELIGION AND CULTURE	137

CONTENTS

UNIT		PAGE
XIX.	ASPECTS OF GENERAL CULTURE	145
XX.	SUBREGIONS OF THE SOUTHEAST	151
XXI.	THE TENNESSEE VALLEY	161
XXII.	STATES AND REGIONS	169
XXIII.	THE SOUTHWEST AND THE SOUTHEAST	177
XXIV.	TOWARDS REGIONAL PLANNING	185
	BOOK LIST FOR SUPPLEMENTARY READING	192
	INDEX OF DEFINITIONS	193

MANUAL FOR SOUTHERN REGIONS

INTRODUCTION TO THE PROGRAM OF STUDY

THIS MANUAL is designed to help any person or group in a factual and penetrating study of the entire South, especially as that region stands in comparison with the rest of the country. Although the southwestern states are generally considered in the southern group, "The South" in this study will refer primarily to the eleven southeastern states.

The basic volume, *Southern Regions*, generally acclaimed as one of the most valuable contributions ever to issue from the South, is the work of its own scholars and citizens. The student will need to have ready access to the book, which contains sufficient study material to keep energetic thinkers busy for many a month, even many years. Its suggestive "leads" are almost limitless. Therefore, no voluminous extra readings are indicated in the units of study; only a few books are given special mention in the Section B of certain assignments and in the list on page 190 of this *Manual*. These few suggested readings provide variation of viewpoint, emphasis, and style. Those who wish still further materials are referred to pages 607-620.[1]

1. UNIT PLAN. The study is divided into units each of which will be introduced by two or three paragraphs that open to view in a general way the substance of the unit with its several sections designated as follows:

- A. Aims for the student
- B. Reading material for study
- C. Definitions and general guidance
- D. Questions primarily on facts and mapograph interpretations
- E. Questions primarily on policy and program
- F. Topics for forum and debate
- G. Suggestions

The questions under D are usually simpler than those under E. The policy and program questions as well as the topics for forum are intended for the more advanced students.

2. RELATION OF *Manual* TO *Southern Regions*. The course of study covers twenty-four units that follow the twenty subheads of Chapter I in

---

[1] All page references henceforth will indicate the basic volume, *Southern Regions*, unless otherwise stated.

Southern Regions. It should be emphasized that this chapter is a syllabus or summary of the other ten chapters. About a dozen numbered paragraphs appear under each subhead in Chapter I. These will be the point of departure since they condense the main factors to be dealt with in more detail in Chapters II-XI. For example, note how paragraphs 46, 47, 48, and 49 are given more detailed discussion on pages 221, 222, and 223.

3. DEFINITIONS. To take care of certain words, terms, and concepts that may be unknown or obscure to the reader, definitions and explanations of the more difficult of these are attempted in Section C of each unit. The earlier units will naturally offer more help in this connection than the later assignments. The dictionary should, of course, always be at hand. Frequent reference to the dictionary and perhaps to the encyclopaedia is to be expected. As in all sciences, a body of words and terms develops that makes for economy of expression and understanding for those who are familiar with the subject matter. However, for those who are new to the study, help will be needed on numerous words and phrases. Without recourse to the dictionary and studious effort throughout, many an important point will be missed. Although words and terms are explained as they appear in the order of study, the "Index of Definitions" at the end of this *Manual* will be useful by indicating the page location of definitions.

4. SCHOOL, COLLEGE, AND CLUB GROUP STUDY. For a rather intensive study program, three hours a week for an entire year will be required. Systematic study at the upper high school level, at the college level, and at the non-academic adult level will require each its own approach, ranging from rather simple to more penetrating treatment. In any case, flexibility is to be desired according to the composition of the study group. Some units will of necessity require more time than others and frequently there may be considerable emphasis in the discussion, perhaps even a seeming over-stress of some point that has awakened lively interest. For a general course emphasizing only the "high spots," three hours a week for fifteen weeks will probably yield fairly satisfactory results.

5. THE TEACHER AND STUDY OF SPECIAL ASPECTS. *The teacher or leader of the study group should plan carefully concerning the quantity of work to be done. More questions and topics are provided than can be adequately handled by the average class. From the standpoint of time and ability it may be advisable to omit certain items in the exercises, with only a few of the simpler questions and topics given out to students for study and report.* To meet certain circumstances and group desires, special study can be arranged by thoughtful leaders and groups. Abbreviated and simplified programs can be provided for almost any age, even for primary school chil-

dren under the resourceful teacher who can readily discern "project" material at a number of points throughout the book, and who can see in the sandpile, garden, and excursions to the countryside ways of introducing to children the simpler aspects of soil erosion, plant growth, and forest preservation. For young and old there is much in *Southern Regions* that can be translated in an interesting manner. Those who conduct groups in special aspects of the study may wish to arrange the work according to the Index on pages 651-664 of *Southern Regions*. For example, glance at page 654, "Education"; or at page 656, the several heads relating to "Industry"; or at page 657, "Negro." In following a study of special phases and their interrelationships, teacher and student should not forget how necessary it is to make cross references. "Education" connects with the "Negro," and each with many other headings.

6. FACT AND MAPOGRAPH QUESTIONS. The maps and charts set forth with remarkable force numerous facts, relationships, comparisons, and trends. For example, a glance at the map on page 38 gives meaning to the statement issued by the United States Department of Agriculture in March 1936: "In terms of money, the direct toll of erosion is estimated at 400 million dollars annually." Again, words and figures alone could not adequately describe the pictures on pages 172, 188, and 216. Given such stark facts, one thinks of the need for a policy and a program. In arranging questions for this *Manual* it was well-nigh impossible to make ever clear distinctions between fact and policy questions.

7. POLICY AND PROGRAM QUESTIONS. Of course, it is interesting and valuable to lay hold on facts, to keep them in mind, but it is more important to understand their meanings, their implications, and the trends that grow out of conditions and situations. But that is not all; something must be done besides getting, understanding, and facing facts. Policies and programs that are progressive and cautious are called for today. Here is the need and the challenge: good leading and good following; patiently, not too hurriedly, the taking of constructive first steps. To obtain facts, to understand their meaning, to face them in the light of present and future needs, and then to do something about them scientifically rather than emotionally—this is the part of wisdom as the study is pursued.

8. THE STUDENT: METHOD AND MIND. Each student will probably have his own special interests in the total subject. A loose-leaf notebook and workbook may be used to advantage to write down, according to one's own preferences and method, those facts or points of discussion that are particularly impressive. Thus, students in groups can exchange ideas profitably as they discuss various aspects of their study.

For the more advanced student to get fruitful results, it will probably be necessary that at least from one to three hours be given to careful preparation of each unit. Some of the longer units will require more than three hours; others will call for less time.

A few pointed, meaningful facts are far better than a great mass of data poorly understood or interpreted. No great effort should be made to commit vast tables, charts, and figures to memory.

The mind kept free will leave little room for notions and prejudices that obscure the light. Two great scientists of modern times have spoken thus:

I have steadily endeavored to keep my mind free so as to give up any hypothesis however much beloved—and I cannot resist forming one on every subject—as soon as facts are shown to be opposed to it. (Darwin.)

What can I wish to the youth of my country who devote themselves to science?

Firstly, gradualness. About this most important condition of fruitful scientific work I never can speak without emotion. Gradualness, gradualness, and gradualness. From the very beginning of your work, school yourselves to severe gradualness in the accumulation of knowledge.

Learn the ABC of science before you try to ascend to its summit. Never begin the subsequent without mastering the preceding. Never attempt to screen an insufficiency of knowledge even by the most audacious surmise and hypothesis. Howsoever this soap-bubble will rejoice your eyes by its play it inevitably will burst and you will have nothing except shame.

School yourselves to demureness and patience. Learn to inure yourselves to drudgery in science. Learn, compare, collect the facts!

Perfect as is the wing of a bird, it never could raise the bird up without resting on air. Facts are the air of a scientist. Without them you never can fly. Without them your "theories" are vain efforts.

But in learning, experimenting, observing, try not to stay on the surface of the facts. Do not become the archivists of facts. Try to penetrate to the secret of their occurrence, persistently search for the laws which govern them.

Secondly, modesty. Never think that you already know all. However highly you are appraised, always have the courage to say of yourself—I am ignorant.

Do not allow haughtiness to take you in possession. Due to that you will be obstinate where it is necessary to agree, you will refuse useful advice and friendly help, you will lose the standard of objectiveness.

Thirdly, passion. Remember that science demands from a man all his life. If you had two lives that would be not enough for you. Be passionate in your work and your searchings. (Written by Pavlov just before his death on February 27, 1936, at the age of eighty-seven years.)

INTRODUCTION

Small wonder that editorials in newspapers and learned journals have acclaimed this bequest of Pavlov one of the most stirring documents that has come to light in a long time.

And now the study begins! May book and mind be kept open and active in the quest for an understanding of the plight and promise of our southern regions.

NOTES

NOTES

NOTES

UNIT I

THE OBJECTIVES OF THE SOUTHERN REGIONAL STUDY

The purpose of the Southern Regional Study is to provide a clear picture of the two southern regions, the Southeast and the Southwest. The Southeast is featured first. Troublesome problems have grown out of historical circumstance and they still remain to afflict the southern area and its people. The liabilities of the total South make the picture rather dark from numerous angles, but there are aspects of the place and the people that indicate brighter, happier years ahead if wise action follows good thinking. At any rate the South does not stand or fall alone.

This fact of interdependence leads to another objective or goal of this study; namely, to show the relationship which the several regions bear to each other and to the country as a whole. The South must be seen in comparison with the other regions and with the entire nation as its setting. Neither the fruits of health and wealth nor the husks of misery and poverty can be for long the monopoly of any group of thinking, active people. The South has wealth, both natural and human, and it has poverty of many kinds; wealth of water, trees, minerals, people of undeveloped abilities; poverty as seen in "marginality," "immaturity," and "cumulative handicaps." Sectionalism, not wholly of the South's own making, is responsible for many of the grievous regional troubles. The constricting influence of sectionalism, whether in New England or the South, prevents the people from seeing themselves or others except in narrow ways of local self-interest. Sectionalism today is less defensible than ever because of the interdependence of region with region as a result of rapid travel and communication, with all that they mean of interchange. Whether we will it or not, the nation is indivisible and must make increasingly available "liberty and justice for all" its people.

A. Aims for the student
1. To become familiar with southern regions and subregions, their boundaries and areas.
2. To take some first steps toward a larger knowledge of the wealth and poverty of the regions.
3. To make some preliminary measurements of responsibility—individual and local, regional and national.

4. To reckon whether design and progress can displace drift and stagnation, and to glimpse consequences of either course.

B. Reading material for study

Southern Regions, Chapter II, pp. 207-217 (read p. 217 first), Chapter I, pp. 1-5. Read and study the book along with the definition and guidance material below in C. Those participating in the program of study are reminded that occasional reference to paragraphs 5, 6, 7, and 8 of the Introduction to the *Manual* may be of guidance in the assignment of questions and topics.

C. Definitions and general guidance

The text pages for this first unit contain a number of words and terms that may be new or vague to people not acquainted with the expressions of social science. Only careful reading and study, the thinking and re-thinking of the larger facts and meanings, will bring satisfactory understanding of the book. The dictionary should always be within reach, and *used*.

The following words and terms are given more or less in the order of their appearance in the assigned chapters.

Culture to the scientist means the whole life of a human group. Wherever man is found, there is culture. All peoples, from the lowliest savage to the highest European or American people, possess culture. Savages have a rather simple culture; twentieth century Euro-American culture is very complex and intricate. Family and educational systems, government and religion, language and art, tools and means of conveyance, ceremonials and traditions—all these are characteristic of humanity but are never found completely among the activities of animals lower than man. Oriental culture as seen in the Chinese and Japanese contrasts with our American ways in speech, dress, food habits, architecture, art, house furnishing, family life, educational systems, marriage and burial customs, sanitation, ancestral traditions, religion, and in a host of other details. Similarly, but far less markedly, there are culture differences between Europe and America and even between the regions of the United States. The South is not like the North in the way it plants its corn and the way it cooks its cornbread. The regions differ in many other unimportant details. It should be clear then that when the word "culture" is used in our study, it means far more than refinement of manners or civilization. By turning to pages 4, 292, 332, 376, 432, 462, and 496, representative lists of culture details can be explored. These culture items are used as indices of measurement and comparison.

Framework is another word met early and frequently. This refers to a total picturization including all possible facts, hundreds of them, and their meaning. This framework would also emphasize the real and the attainable rather than the ideal, the wishful, and the impracticable. It would depict long-time views and patience, sure rather than hasty reform. In other words, this Southern Regional Study frames a mosaic of many pieces presenting what is and what may be as a result of the application of common sense. The picture must be viewed clearly, unemotionally, *as it is* and not through the colored glasses of excuse-making, rationalization, and romanticism. In comparing state with state, region with region, the "happy medium" rather than the "vivid extremes" should be kept in mind.

Rationalization: Concocting plausible or "good" (?) reasons rather than real ones to account for beliefs or behavior, especially when these plausible reasons are challenged; or in other words, the dressing up of unworthy motives in the garb of justification.

Folk-regional society is an all-inclusive term. We all know that tradition, habit, and the place where people live have a strong tendency to give that people a distinctiveness as compared with other peoples. The South had Negroes, slavery, and cotton plantations. The North and the West developed by reason of different land forms, usages, and traditions. While similar in the main, religion, family life, education, industry, and government differ in detail from region to region. The folk themselves are both cause and effect of these regional differences. The maps and charts throughout the book indicate these folk-regional differences interestingly. Consult, for example, pages 140, 146, 172, 188, 216, and 346.

Demography has to do with population distribution, including not only the statistical features such as rates of birth, marriage, death, and health, but also the social causes and consequences of population trends. (See Unit VI for fuller definition.)

Sectionalism is mentioned on page 2 of the book as an affliction of the Southeast. This refers to the old separatism of the ante-bellum South, and is opposed to regionalism. Other parts of the country have not escaped the drag-effect of sectionalism which tends to spend itself in looking backward, in idealization of the past, and in stressing satisfaction and complacency especially in political, economic, religious, and social traditions. Sectionalism also grabs for future advantage. (See pp. 253-259.)

Regionalism as opposed to sectionalism, comprehends the southern culture and economy as an integral part *of* the nation rather than separate *from* it. It connects with realism, things as they are, and faces forward to meet conditions squarely in the modern scientific manner, planning next steps rather than drifting in old channels. The land and the people are not the same yesterday, today, and forever. The essential contrast between sectionalism and regionalism is one of stagnation on the one hand and movement on the other. (See pp. 253-259.)

The inference is that the Southeast has tended to settle down almost proudly and boastfully into the stagnation of localism and sectionalism. Another inference is that it is time to climb.

The foregoing definitions and explanations refer mostly to pages 1-5. The next listing deals with words and expressions found between pages 207 and 217.

Multiple subregions: Glance at pages 152 to 162. These will be discussed further in Unit XX.

Realism and idealism: Facing facts and seeing things as they really are in a very imperfect human society as compared with looking hopefully, wishfully toward the ideal, or as things might be in a perfect society.

Marginality describes that which is near the edge or barely "getting by," as when there is scarcity and poverty of soil, food, schools, books; little or no art, music, and other good things of life. Submarginality would then mean below the level of marginality. (See Unit XX.)

Immaturity as it is used in the book connotes more than mere lack of age. An individual or a people, even though advanced in years, may not have "grown up"; may still be childish in desires and behavior; may react physically, even brutishly, instead of maturely and intellectually (civilization has not yet matured, else it would not war upon itself); may be unable to see or imagine tomorrow or next year in the light of today's thinking and acting. The hopeful implication would be that there is still time to mature.

Cultural pathology: Pathology refers to disease. Human groups, like the individual, can be in bad health, even diseased. Poverty, for example, has been described as a sore on the body of society; war, as a cancer eating at the vitals of civilization.

Functional analysis: Function always means action. A school or church may have a fine structure or edifice, but how about the functioning; what is the school or church actually doing? To study or analyze what a person or an institution or a region is doing is far more important and valuable than to give much attention to outward structure.

Time quality refers to the rôle of time along with geography and other environmental factors in the making of culture. It refers to *how* time is used rather than to how much is used; has to do with speed or slowness, acceleration or lag, keeping up or falling behind. In view of the South's handicaps, its present gait, and the needs of the future, has it lost time, and will it lose in the days ahead? Quality of use is more important than quantity. (The time quality of Japan's material advancement in the last fifty

OBJECTIVES OF THE STUDY

years has been remarkable.) A high quality of accomplishment by the South in the years immediately ahead will correct some of the former losses.

Priority schedules would include things to be done in the order of their importance or adoption in a plan. Soil saving and restoration would come prior to almost everything else in a long schedule of needs. High in the list also would be new types of farming and a more mature evaluation of the importance of education.

Quartile: A statistical term referring to the division of the total hundred per cent into quarters. Any long list of comparable items such as the ages of people, the number of public libraries, the crop production, the acres of farm land, the miles of paved road, the number of churches, the number of mob uprisings, and any other cultural items that can be listed can be compared by regions, states, or counties. When these lists are arranged in order for any culture item, it is possible to see almost at a glance how a region or a state compares with other regions or states. The South is in the lowest 25 per cent (first quartile) in milk production, and in the highest 25 per cent of all the regions (fourth quartile) in tobacco production. Then, if any such array of percentaged items is divided into quarters, the topmost is called the fourth quartile (Q_4); the 25 per cent coming between 50 per cent and 75 per cent, the third quartile (Q_3); the 25 per cent between 25 per cent and 50 per cent, the second quartile (Q_2); and the lowest 25 per cent, the first quartile. See, for example, pages 72, 320, and 322. (In a few instances, notably page 98, the ordering of the quartiles was reversed by mistake. Here the black should mean the first or lowest quartile and the white, the fourth or highest.)

Median: A measure of average; the point at which 50 per cent of a list or array is above and 50 per cent is below; the dividing line between the second and third quartiles.

Now the reader is prepared to understand one of the most striking pages in the book, page 216, reproduced as page 26 in this *Manual*. In brief, it says the southern states are at the bottom of the list in practically every instance, no matter what the item of comparison nor how the score is computed. It should be noted that the map deals with twenty-three cultural tables which should not be confused with the 152 tabulated cultural items on the lower half of the page, which again is only an uncritical selection from the total seven hundred used in the book. For a discussion of the table, see the last paragraph on page 241. Education, health, and wealth, are three of the twenty-three cultural tables which made this map. Suppose the State of Washington is compared with Georgia as representing two states distant from each other. How remarkable is the contrast? Compare the six regions with each other. Glance at question 11 under D in this first unit. Which group or groups in the dozen listed would likely be most keenly aware of the real condition in the South as shown on page 216? Which group would be inclined to respond with a regional rather than with a local enthusiasm to a program of rebuilding the whole South?

D. **Questions primarily on facts and mapograph interpretations**
   1. Name the regions with which *Southern Regions* deals. How many are southern? How many states does each southern region include?
   2. In which one of the twenty-seven subregions (p. 152) do you live?
   3. In which subregion has there been the greatest population increase for the years 1920-1930? Explain the increase.
   4. How does the South rank with regard to population, wealth, area, and farm land (p. 208)? How good or convincing is a measure that deals merely with quantity? What else must be considered?
   5. What is "natural wealth"? "Human wealth"? How valuable is one without the other?
   6. Study the four maps on the right-hand side of page 214 and describe the trend and present situation with regard to the number of white children under five years of age between 1880 and 1930. What special problems arise where there are large numbers of children?
   7. Indicate the different evidences of "marginality" and "immaturity" in the following maps: pages 38, 172, 188, 240, 346, 348, 516, and 518.
   8. Would you agree that the maps on pages 146 and 490 indicate "cultural pathology"? Why?
   9. What is there in southern life that justifies the reference on page 1 to "complexity of culture"? Give examples.
   10. What is there in southern life that justifies the reference on page 1 to "cumulative handicaps"? Give examples.
   11. Which group would be the most likely to make a fair and all-inclusive study of a region:

industrialists	landlords
tenants	lawyers
newspaper editors	clergymen
bankers	university researchers
real estate promoters	chambers of commerce
politicians	novelists

   In answering, arrange your list in the order of what you consider their reliability and freedom from bias, the most reliable at the top and the least reliable

OBJECTIVES OF THE STUDY

at the bottom, and indicate why you consider some of them more reliable than others.

E. Questions primarily on policy and program

1. In what important ways are the Southeast and the Southwest most alike? Most different? How do these similarities and differences relate to the future development of each region?
2. What is a demagogue? Is there anything in the southern situation that encourages the growth of demagoguery? Will the South of tomorrow need a different type of leadership? Illustrate.
3. What can you detect on page 2, paragraph 9, that suggests the need of a new definition of responsibility involving the individual, the community, the county, the state, the region, the nation, and other nations?
4. By stressing the need for reintegration and national participation (pp. 1 and 599) the book implies that the South has been a victim of sectionally-minded exploiters from outside. How true is this and what evidence is there?
5. Why does the book argue that the problem of the South is a national problem?
6. A six to twelve-year period of achieving definite changes and improvements that will mean national and regional progress is recommended. From your knowledge and study thus far, what would you say must and can be done in that length of time?

F. Topics for debate and forum

1. "The South, when it shall have succeeded, will have more than itself to thank, and if it fails, unfortunately more than itself to blame" (p. 209).
2. A rightward movement is necessary and desirable to save the South. (Paragraph beginning at the bottom of page 211 and ending on page 213. See also top of page 217.)
3. Nobody ever starves in the South, anyway.
4. The Bible supports the belief that there always will be shiftless poor people, and we should resign ourselves to this fact.
5. If people were not so poor they would not be so shiftless.
6. In view of its present problems, the South cannot at the same time both pride itself about the past and prod itself into progress.

G. Suggestions for this unit

This first unit should cover two class periods of one hour each. The questions on policy and program, and the topics for debate and forum should not be assigned unless class members are capable of working them up satisfactorily.

Thorough work is necessary in all units, particularly with this first one.

Serious subject matter demands serious attention by the leader and all members of the study group whether the class is made up of college students taking a required course or whether it is a community club class on a voluntary basis.

NOTES

NOTES

UNIT II

GEOGRAPHIC FACTORS AND PHYSICAL SETTING

Now that the study program has been approached through a consideration of objectives, the next step is to present that foundation material upon which can be erected a structure of knowledge, thinking, and action. Geographic study is important because people are understood very largely in terms of the place where they live. The earth came before man; it sets limits to what he is and does; it supports and sustains him. Geographic environment gives man abundant materials, but it does not tell him what to do with them. That has to be learned.

Physical resources may be unknown or neglected, or they may be abused rather than properly used. For example, minerals and waterpower were here in the western hemisphere before explorers and settlers came in the sixteenth and seventeenth centuries, but very little was done about rich American resources until European white culture mined and manufactured them. The simple culture of the North American Indian was not adequate to make large use of the riches beneath, above, and around him. Therefore, to understand a people it is necessary to look into their cultural heritage. This cultural feature of regional study—to be examined in the third unit—should be kept somewhat in mind as the geographic aspects are studied in this present unit.

The study now reveals what has long been needed, a revised picture of the South, and answers the question: What is southern likeness or uniformity from state to state; in other words, what is southern homogeneity? The old lumping of states from Texas to Maryland and from Florida to Missouri as "South" is no longer accurate. The Southeastern States differ from the Southwestern States in many details, important and unimportant. The Southeast contains eleven states with twenty-five or thirty subdivisions. It will be shown that the Southeast has many attributes, much variety in soil, climate, and general physical fitness for living that is of the best. The climate is thought by some to be unfavorable to the highest mental efficiency in otherwise fertile areas, or subregions.

It is emphasized here, as frequently throughout the book, that geographic factors and conditions do much to shape the ways of the people. The highland dweller differs from the plainsman; the heavily-clad northerner from the habitant of the warmer clime; altitude, temperature, land forms, conditions of moisture, soil fertility and productivity—all have an influence upon the people.

A. Aims for the student
1. To locate the real and homogeneous South of today by using many culture items or indices of measurement.
2. To show that several states have either lost their earlier or assumed "southernness" or are now losing it.
3. To suggest that "the Southeast possesses an extraordinary number of those geographic attributes which constitute the optimum setting for economic achievement and cultural adequacy." (See definitions in C.)
4. To consider briefly the influence of southeastern geography upon the people.

B. Reading material for study
Southern Regions, Chapter I, pp. 5-11; Chapter II, pp. 219, 233-235; Chapter IV, pp. 291-299.[1]

Suggested additional reading: *Human Geography of the South*, by Rupert B. Vance, Chapter II.

C. Definitions and general guidance
Dynamics: This means activity and change as contrasted with that which is static or stationary and slow to change. Some cultures, regions, and peoples are more dynamic than others. Dynamics and statics have to do with ideas as well as things.

Workable techniques: Practical ways and means of accomplishing something.

Optimum setting: The best or most advantageous situation.

Dominance of characteristics: Prominence or emphasis of things or ideas. Cotton, tobacco, and corn; farm tenancy, racial segregation, many churches, few libraries; poverty, much church attendance, little reading; sentiments of loyalty, habits of courtesy, abundance of hospitality—all are dominant characteristics of the South.

D. Questions primarily on facts and mapograph interpretations
1. Why is it permissible to consider hogs, lynchings, illiteracy, disease types, and death rates among cultural indices of measurement?
2. Why is it inaccurate to speak of "the South" when one is thinking of Maryland and Missouri? (Study p. 8.) Where do Texas and Oklahoma belong?

---

[1] Later units will deal further with the regional-geographic advantages of the southeastern region. Also the Southeast and the Southwest will be studied further in Unit XXIII.

GEOGRAPHIC AND PHYSICAL FACTORS

3. Why are Louisiana and Arkansas Southeast rather than Southwest? (Study p. 10.)
4. If Maryland and Missouri were to be included in the southeastern region, how would it affect the general picture of the total region?
5. Examine the six indices illustrated by maps on page 176.
    a. Is Virginia leaning toward or away from the Southeast?
    b. Is Kentucky leaning toward or away from the Southeast?
    c. Are Tennessee, North Carolina, and Louisiana leaning slightly away from the Southeast?
    d. What states are indisputably southeastern in these six farm indices?
    e. How do you explain Florida in this connection?
6. Which of the following would you consider illustrative of the "dynamics of the emerging southwestern region," and why?
    a. Automobile manufacturing
    b. Water power
    c. Oil resources and processing
    d. Leadership in science
    e. Mechanized cotton production
7. Evaluate some of the advantageous geographic attributes of the Southeast.
8. Have you observed anything about rainfall that may not be favorable? Explain.
9. The northern farmhouse, snug to the ground; huge, orderly woodpile; long winters; deep snow, shorter growing season; home ownership; long school terms; village libraries; town meetings. What differences would you expect to find between the people of the northern farm and those of a typical southern farm, because of geography? (Refer to pp. 219 and 235.)
10. How is culture measured and compared? Illustrate from the book.

E. Questions primarily on policy and program

1. What is meant by "southern homogeneity"? In a regional plan why not consider all the states below the Mason-Dixon line as "The South"?
2. Is it likely that geography will connect fairly directly with the movement of an industry from one region to another? Is this the explanation of the shift from North to South of cotton manufacturing? Explain.
3. From the standpoint of land utilization and agricultural policy, are the facts on pages 40 and 66 good or bad? Why? What has geography to offer by way of explaining this fertilizer problem?
4. Were the original state lines laid out according to geographic and regional needs or were they "historical accidents"? Is it time to consider regional functioning rather than follow inflexibly traditional boundaries? Why, or why not? (Glance at the maps between pp. 252 and 270.)
5. Can you see a cycle of southern adversity and deficiency in the statement: As

the soil is, so the people are; as the soil becomes, so the people will be? Go into considerable detail in rounding out the cycle as you see it.

F. Topics for debate and forum
1. The South possesses geographic riches amid cultural poverty.
2. Geographic factors are related to public opinion and legislation. (For example, consider the highland counties of states like North Carolina and Alabama and Tennessee as compared with their lowland counties in valleys and on the coast.)
3. The Southeast is handicapped by relatively poor soil in the areas with the best climatic conditions and by relatively poor climate in the areas with the most productive soil.
4. The South has too much rainfall to be a first-class farming country.

G. Suggestions for this unit

This unit, shorter than Unit I, should require less class time, probably one period. Due emphasis should be given to factual content so that social, economic, and political meaning is derived from the study.

NOTES

NOTES

NOTES

RANK OF STATES BASED ON TWENTY-THREE CULTURAL TABLES

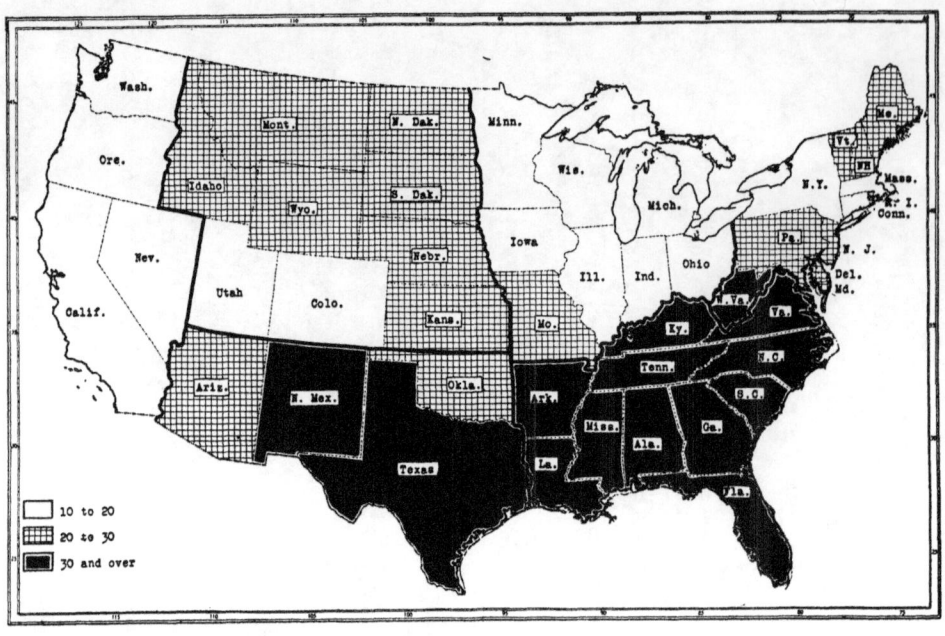

10 to 20
20 to 30
30 and over

STATE QUARTILE DISTRIBUTION IN 152 CULTURAL ITEMS

STATE AND REGION	Number of Times in Lowest Quartile	Number of Times Outside the Lowest Quartile	Number of Times in the Highest Quartile	STATE AND REGION	Number of Times in Lowest Quartile	Number of Times Outside the Lowest Quartile	Number of Times in the Highest Quartile
Southeast	89	63	15	*Middle States*	15	137	40
Virginia	62	90	11	Ohio	13	139	34
North Carolina	79	73	27	Indiana	13	139	24
South Carolina	107	45	13	Illinois	13	139	57
Georgia	114	38	10	Michigan	8	144	52
Florida	56	96	30	Wisconsin	12	140	38
Kentucky	88	64	10	Minnesota	13	139	40
Tennessee	78	74	7	Iowa	23	129	59
Alabama	104	48	13	Missouri	22	130	17
Mississippi	104	48	21				
Arkansas	111	41	10	*Northwest*	26	126	39
Louisiana	76	76	14	North Dakota	40	112	45
				South Dakota	28	124	42
Southwest	45	107	23	Nebraska	23	129	51
Oklahoma	39	113	15	Kansas	15	137	38
Texas	45	107	17	Montana	33	119	32
New Mexico	65	87	18	Idaho	34	118	25
Arizona	30	122	41	Wyoming	24	128	50
				Colorado	12	140	34
Northeast	24	128	46	Utah	23	129	38
Maine	31	121	26				
New Hampshire	30	122	44	*Far West*	16	136	68
Vermont	28	124	37	Nevada	24	128	66
Massachusetts	16	136	78	Washington	10	142	54
Rhode Island	20	132	51	Oregon	13	139	60
Connecticut	17	135	72	California	15	137	93
New York	15	137	70				
New Jersey	21	131	61				
Delaware	33	119	26				
Pennsylvania	12	140	35				
Maryland	13	139	32				
West Virginia	48	104	19				

See representative list of indices on pp. 4, 292, 332, 376, 432, 462, 496. The above table makes no allowance for refined or weighted indices. It represents only a common mode of comparison which indicates in a broad way conventional measures of the contrast between physical resources and cultural reality.

Reprinted from page 216 in *Southern Regions*.

UNIT III

CULTURAL EQUIPMENT AND HISTORICAL BACKGROUNDS

It is fairly well established that geographic setting has large influence on what people do, how they think, what prejudices and traditions they cherish, how they legislate, how they look upon the ways of government and law, church and religion, education and literacy, crime and race relations, and a host of other things that make up the cultural equipment of a people. Yet it has been indicated that precisely there is no single South; there are many Souths. Boundary lines that coincide with rivers or mountain ridges or that result from decisions of early surveyors do not insure oneness of the people residing within those boundaries today. It is true also that the South of romance and tradition does not necessarily conform to the larger South of many subregions that outlines itself when hundreds of culture items of comparison are employed from state to state. It can be said with some conclusiveness that the ways of a people are determined by the combined influences of geography, history, and their own culture.

In this third unit consideration is given to the cultural equipment of the southern regions and to the historical backgrounds that have so much to do with the place and people of today. The great body of any people's culture comes cumulatively out of history with only a few new ideas and changes welcomed from generation to generation. Material invention and change are, of course, accepted much more readily than social invention. Electric lights were quickly adopted in our cities, but social inventions such as, for example, the city manager or the county manager, are accepted very slowly.

Culture tends to become organized around certain ideas and sentiments in which vested interests play no small part. The "ganging together" of the traditions may mean a solid front to preserve the old and resist the new in race relations, religion, politics, education, economics, farming methods, and family patterns. Dr. Odum has this in mind when he refers to "unthinking mass assumptions and uncritical judgments."

A. Aims for the student
  1. To try some critical thinking and viewing of southern culture and history, remembering that criticism can be both positive and negative.
  2. To evaluate loyalty and patriotism as they appear against a background of

pressing modern needs in the fields of religion, politics, labor, agriculture, industry, and race.
3. To look through the microscope of self-analysis today and examine the tissues and cells of southern life as it relates to the nation, and then ask ourselves: "What should and what can be done about it?"
4. To stimulate thinking that points to action on the major crises of the regions.

B. Reading material for study

Southern Regions: Chapter I, pp. 11-15; Chapter II, pp. 225-235; Chapter V, pp. 287-290.

Suggested additional reading: *Culture in the South*, the work of some thirty southerners under the editorship of W. T. Couch. Chapter II and others deserve study.

I'll Take My Stand, by Twelve Southerners, presents some interesting arguments.

C. Definitions and general guidance

Incidence: A coincidence of circumstances, unpredictable, lying somewhere between luck and accident and predestined purpose which exerts great influence on the destinies of men and peoples. *Southern Regions* refers to historical, regional, geographic, and other types of incidence. Broadly speaking the boll weevil, the migration of Negroes, the coming of the mechanical cotton picker, soil erosion—all these are among the aspects of "social incidence" that might be defined as "regional incidence" also.

Dichotomy, dichotomous: Cutting in two; division; branching or forking, usually in a continued series of sub-groupings.

Quality characteristics: The English, for example, are noted for their trained statesmen, law and order, and mature democracy; the Japanese for their quick adaptability, energy, and willingness to work hard; the New Englander for his frugality and efficiency; the Southerner for his gentility, friendliness, and hospitality. These are, of course, positive and advantageous "quality characteristics" against which might be listed some negative and undesirable qualities. Some quality characteristics are imagined or largely mythical rather than actual.

Patterns: This word has a great many connections. Dressmakers and foundrymen certainly have no monopoly in its use. People have habit patterns, speech patterns, action patterns. Groups likewise have their behavior patterns which are followed more or less without question by most individuals. The general pattern of southern life is much like that of other regions, but when we examine the threads we find considerable difference within states, between states, and between regions. (See *Culture* as defined in Unit I.)

EQUIPMENT AND BACKGROUNDS

Culture (or cultural) inbreeding: Inbreeding means to breed with that which is closely related, or like with like. A people or region, seemingly satisfied with its ways and condition, may ignore or reject the incoming of ideas and methods from outside even though these importations would be of benefit. China is an example of resistance to outside things, a case of cultural inbreeding involving millions of folk and thousands of years, with religion, education, health, economics, and countless other things practically unchanged from century to century. Who has not heard of a board of education that insisted upon having "one of our own folks," regardless of qualifications (rather than have an outsider), for a superintendent or teacher in the school system? Turn to page 525, paragraph beginning: "The folkways of southern politics. . . ."

Culture (or cultural) lag: This refers to the unevenness of advance in culture. Some aspects of culture, usually the materialistic, forge ahead while others, especially the non-materialistic, commonly thought of as the social and spiritual, lag behind. For illustration: our transportation systems are modern; inventions are eagerly applied to improve means of travel by land or sea or air. But consider the reluctance and slowness of change in politics, education, ways of religion, and in many other departments of our life where it would appear that we are still "horse-and-buggy" minded, if not "ox-cart" or stubbornly "mulish" in our methods. Is there evidence of culture lag in the fact that many of our states have several times as many expensive, wasteful, county seats and sitting officials as are needed? (See Unit X.)

Societal evolution: Society, like the earth itself, undergoes developmental change. Man's ideas and values become altered as time passes. What was suitable and "right" yesterday may be unsuitable and "wrong" today and tomorrow. Man once moved about in mountain caves; now he moves mountains of rock to build skyscrapers. Once he took almost everything he wanted by force; now he trades, negotiates, and uses persuasion. The Old Testament pictures little children being killed as sacrifices by their Moloch-worshipping parents; then step by step strode the great prophets and teachers unfolding truth through the centuries until in 1912 we see the men of the steamship *Titanic* stepping aside that women and children might be saved. Society evolves!

D. Questions primarily on facts and mapograph interpretations
1. When someone mentions "the North" to you, what comes first and most prominently to your mind? "The West"? "The Deep South"?
2. Illustrate what is meant by an "uncritical judgment"?

3. What is likely to be wrong about "mass assumptions"? How much do you find your own assumptions to be changing as you study and travel and meet people from other regions?
4. Illustrate what is meant by a "frontier pattern." (See p. 15, paragraph 36.)
5. What is a regional "crisis"? (Think out your own answer or answers, then list those mentioned on pp. 13 and 219.)
6. Can you think of any further crises that might be considered in terms of climate and topography? How recent are they and of what nature?
7. Which of the great crises afflicting the South, past and present, seem to you to be most serious, and why?
8. List a few "outmoded patterns" and "loyalties" to the past. Should any of these be retained or should they be discarded?
9. Has any group or organization a right to exist if it does nothing more than glorify past events in a sentimental manner? What is it that justifies the existence of any organization?
10. Is like-mindedness a wholly good thing for politics, religion, race relations, farm methods, patriotism, and economic traditions? Why or why not?
11. What new classes and labor relations arose when industry came South? What habits of mind and tendencies to label things and people uncritically, have become almost traditional in the South?
12. Must there always be a tenant problem? Why?
13. Must the "Negro problem" always be a dual drain upon resources in the South? Upon what resources? Why, how, when, if ever a change?
14. Illustrate in what ways the South has been
    a. Isolated
    b. Individualistic
    c. Patriotically ingrown
15. Illustrate in what ways the South has been
    a. Culturally inbred
    b. Politically immature
    c. Socially inadequate
16. Are the blackness and whiteness of the maps on page 12 due to Negro-white conditions from region to region, or to other factors? Explain.
17. Study the maps on page 14. Why does the South rank so low in immigrant folks? Can you see how the literacy test of 1917 for foreign-born immigrants is related to Negro migration?
18. Study the maps on page 228. What caution is necessary in describing a county as submarginal?

E. **Questions primarily on policy and program**
1. Think of a few "quality characterizations" commonly assumed to be superior in the South. How do you know they are superior? What are the founda-

tions of your judgment or measurement? How reliable are these bases of judgment?
2. The culture and history of the country as a whole have been afflicted by prejudice and unscientific customs. In what parts of the total culture of the South have these afflictions or burdens been most heavy and unyielding? Are the problems separable or apart from each other? How? Wherein lies the remedy for each burden or problem?
3. How true is it that in view of all the research and plans for soil and water conservation very little seems to have been accomplished in various parts of the country? The question has been asked of Uncle Sam: "Which shall it be, plan-active con*serv*ation or buck-passing con*vers*ation?" In other words, talk rather than action. How does this question relate to the culture and history of the region and the nation?
4. In his book *Catastrophe and Social Change*, S. H. Prince makes the point that in an emergency or crisis which old ways and methods are inadequate to meet, new methods and points of view assert themselves. (He illustrates how hardened conservatism yielded in Halifax, Nova Scotia, after the terrible disaster of 1917.) A calamity and perhaps an invention may compel a people to see things in a new light. Regardless of the ultimate technical perfection of the Rust cotton picker (see newspapers and magazines of early September, 1936, and later reports), what is unique about the inventors' program in the "cotton crisis"? Are they wisely setting an historical precedent? How necessary is it for this uniqueness to become the accepted practice, especially in crises?
5. The boll weevil, the newly invented cotton picker, recent loss by the United States of international cotton supremacy, industrial and farm labor uprisings—would all these be illustrative of "regional incidence" in connection with cotton culture? Why? How would you illustrate "historical background" in connection with cotton? Illustrate "regional incidence" with regard to soil.
6. Why do so many individuals and governments wait until disaster hangs over or falls upon them before they move into action? (An Italian village refused to move, "stayed put," with a mountain about to blot it out.)
7. Can you see any difference between the demagoguery of the southern politician and the northern politician, especially as you consider the people, the "social soil" into which they dig for votes? (*Harper's* in recent years will be a fruitful supplementary source of reading for this question. See, for example, the September, 1936, issue on the political situation in Massachusetts.)

F. Topics for debate and forum
  1. More libraries will mean less lynching. (Study maps on pp. 146, 188, and 232.)

2. The southern industrialist is justified in his fears of such things as labor unions and collective bargaining. Is the ground for this fear the same as that upon which the politician builds his vote-getting and patronage-dispensing power? (Glance at p. 98; the order of the quartiles should be reversed, with the southern states designated as the first or worst quartile.)
3. The viewpoint of *I'll Take My Stand* is both desirable and practicable.
4. If "cumulative regional characteristics" including "frontier patterns" mean the taking of religion, race relations, politics, and liquor "hard," then the hope of progress is to be found in more flexibility and less hardness.
5. As a special exercise consider paragraph 37 on page 15 as your outline, and construct a short speech that you might give before a civics or community club, wherein you would illustrate simply and clearly: resources, science and skills, culture, and trends.

G. Suggestions for this unit

The items defined under C by no means cover all the new words and concepts that the average student will encounter. The dictionary will make plain what is meant by "crisis," "local autonomy," and other such expressions. When supplementary reading is done in this or in any unit, the reporting of it may be advantageously divided between various members of the group. Main points and arguments should be noted and a time limit set for each participant.

NOTES

NOTES

UNIT IV

EMERGING CULTURE PROBLEMS AND SITUATIONS

In this as in the preceding unit, the study of problems will continue, this time with an eye to standards. The numbered paragraphs in Chapter I give a long list of situations that call for study, for planning, and for action. It will be impossible to deal with all these problems in this unit, but we shall touch most of them. Those not considered now will be studied later.

"There must surely be room enough in the regional cultures of America for experimentation, for exploration, for the genuine liberalism that strives to maintain a quality civilization in a quantity world," writes Dr. Odum on page 237. How remarkably this contrasts with the blatant words of the politician quoted on page 289 of *Liberalism in the South*, by Virginius Dabney, the book suggested for additional reading in this unit. A member of the Georgia legislature proclaims that the only books worth reading are the Bible, the hymnal, and the almanac: "These are enough for anyone," says the legislator. "Read the Bible. It teaches you how to act. Read the hymn-book. It contains the finest poetry ever written. Read the almanac. It shows you how to figure out what the weather will be. There isn't another book that is necessary for anyone to read, and therefore I am opposed to all libraries." Where would we be today if those historic figures who made printing possible—including the printing of Bibles, hymn-books, and almanacs—had been content with such a formula of sufficiency? Some demagogues would defend rather than strive to correct such insufficiency as that depicted on page 118. Why?

It is evident that there is a "chasm between reality and possibility." To bridge this chasm there must be special regional planning based upon the realities of the region and its needs. "Sometime, somewhere, somehow, the nation is accustomed to embark on new adventures and epochs; the present is such a period."

A warning is sounded, as on page 239, about being misled by crude comparisons. In many of these, to be sure, the South shows up to great disadvantage. More important for the South than mere comparison is the matter of steady growth and progress. The danger lies in standing still or slipping backward and scarcely being aware of it. This the South has been doing for too long. However, it will be seen before the study is finished that the South has been moving up and forward in some important ways.

A. Aims for the student
1. To view some aspects of the chasm that lies between the South that is and the South that might be.
2. To test for high or low living standards or levels of existence by comparisons between state and state, and region and region.
3. To be watchful for evidences of constructive change and progress in problems and situations.
4. To venture some first steps in thinking toward planning for remedial action in connection with the most critical problems.

B. Reading material for study
Southern Regions, Chapter I, pp. 15-22; Chapter II, pp. 235-244; and various other pages as indicated in the questions.

Suggested additional reading: *Liberalism in the South*, by Virginius Dabney.

C. Definitions and general guidance
As a few more items are listed for definition and expansion, it should be emphasized that one of the best ways to understand the meaning of unfamiliar word usages and turns of phrase is to study them in their context. Take "regional denominator," for example, as it appears in the middle of page 237. The meaning here is much clearer as seen in the discussion than it would be if dislodged and defined by itself. Again we point out that only a few of the numerous words and terms are set forth for special mention. Study, good thinking, good leadership, group discussion, and the dictionary will suffice for the average student, and hence leave little that is obscure.

Reactionaries: Those who cling hotly to old ideas and ways at all costs, who face backward, who would crucify new leadership, whose fervor burns up perspective in such fields as religion, education, race relations, industry, government, and agriculture.

Conservatives: Those who tend to cling to the old, who stand pat, who warmly defend things as they are or have been, but who do not boil over with hostility toward the new.

Liberals: In general those who fight for the freedom of speech, worship, experimentation. They are, therefore, usually those who admit the need for change and who are inclined to give preference to the new and progressive.

Radicals: Those who are at the opposite extreme from the reactionaries.

The radical wants drastic change, sometimes is willing to indulge in violent overthrow in a desire to discard old ways and principles.

The reactionary is inclined to label the liberal as a radical, and the radical often thinks of the conservative as a reactionary.

The great Aristotle recommended the "golden mean," perhaps in our day to be found in happy combination of sane conservatism and liberalism. Labels are dangerous, frequently false, and usually fragmentary.

Composite products: Suppose we clarify this by illustration. Take, for example, "deficiency of diet." This is made up of many things and factors, including the cash-crop-tenancy habit that has discouraged variety in garden produce and has hindered the utilization of milk cattle. This in turn has encouraged the over-use of commercial fertilizer. Cattle pests have come along to foster still further a "what's-the-use" attitude and hostility toward the government inspector with his "new-fangled" dipping vats. It must be admitted that some people "don't care" about taking care of themselves or of property. So milk and beef have been scarce. Further, cows need care and regular milking, while pigs may roam more freely. Hence, bacon fat and pork become a mainstay; beef and milk in the diet something that for large families is too expensive. Result: malnutrition and pellagra found in the South as in no other region of the nation. Add to this the short school year; few years of schooling; limited health programs or none at all. So the listing might go on and on, almost endlessly, showing many items, "composite products," and *cumulative handicaps* that make for dietary deficiency and human inadequacy—multiple causes leading to multiple related effects.

Abundance potentialities, deficiency actualities: The illustration of composite products applies here. The South has abundant land for pasturing livestock but is tragically deficient in so using it. (See p. 348.) The land and the people could be enriched (potentiality) but are in a state of poverty (actuality).

Objective measures: This implies the measuring of a situation free from prejudice or subjective error. The book and study center around many objective measures of comparison, state to state and region to region. The maps, charts, and tables reveal backwardness and advance as surely as the motion picture camera and the photo-electric cell disclose the finish on the race track. It is the task of social science to apply reliable and objective measures and methods in the human realm where emotion, sentiment, opinion, and prejudice so easily interfere with objectivity.

Marginal subsistence refers to living conditions just above the poverty-deprivation line but far below the comfort level of living.

Submarginal deficiency means that living conditions are below the poverty line, that the necessities of life are so meager and reduced as to make efficiency impossible.

Regimen means order or system in procedure, especially in connection with diet, hygiene, etc.

Norm: The rule or standard or pattern; the normal.

Reintegration: Bringing back unity or wholeness to a thing or situation that is piecemeal, scattered, or separated.

Cumulative emergency: The piling up of serious conditions and problems that aggravate each other and call for remedial attention. The cotton economy, eroded land, and tenant poverty of the South; the housing situation, dilapidation, and congestion in some of our modern cities are examples —cotton tenancy and city slums in each case a cumulative emergency and increasingly in a state of collapse.

Inter-regional optima points to inter-regional "bests." For example, a region that produces a high grade of cotton and low grade tobacco should specialize on cotton and leave tobacco for such areas as grow it better, and vice versa. The Southeast must face this matter with regard to its cotton production in some of its subregions.

D. Questions primarily on facts and mapograph interpretations

1. Where does your state rank in each of the eight columns in the list on page 502? In order to raise your state's ranking what two or three first steps do you think should be taken?
2. What do you see in the map, page 20, that illustrates part of paragraph 40, page 17? Is this the cause or the effect of erosion?
3. What has been happening to leadership in the South? Has there been what might be called an erosion of good leadership? (Refer also to pp. 149-150.)
4. Compare the map on page 568, upper half, with the map on page 346 and draw your own conclusions.
5. Compare paragraph 43, page 17, with lists and discussions on pages 338-339. Do you see any "chasm" between production and consumption? How do you think it can be bridged?
6. Can you state the difference between a "standard of living" and a "level of living"? Which of the two is more the result of drift and habit? How can standards be raised and followed by the mass of the people?
7. Would you use the numbers of radios, automobiles, and cigarettes consumed as a measure of the standard of living, or would you use other culture items? Explain.
8. Should the South be looked upon and treated by Uncle Sam as a poor relative or as an area of battle needing reinforcements? Why?

EMERGING CULTURE PROBLEMS

9. Is there any suggestion in paragraph 52, page 21, that a nation, like a chain, can be no stronger than its weakest part? Explain.
10. In what ways are "dichotomies" costly?
11. What are some of the chief objections to the cash-crop farming practice? How can they be overcome?

E. Questions primarily on policy and program
1. Which one or two of the expensive "dichotomies" could most easily be corrected? Why do you think so? How would you proceed to bring about improvement?
2. Why must some new industries, a new kind of agriculture, and a reforestation program be applied to the South very soon?
3. Can you explain some of the underlying factors affecting the textile industry in recent years, factors having to do with types of people, regional changes, level of living, etc.? Note what has happened in the textile industry between 1919 and 1929. (See p. 70.)
4. Can you link up the following maps in such a way as to explain the statement at the top of page 241? Consult maps on pages 98, 100, 102, 104, 240, and note that the map on page 516 represents membership in the Association of American Universities which stands for high grade scholarship.
5. What sort of an educational strain or tension do you see between a high birth rate and a low income or wealth rate for the southern regions? What sooner or later must relieve this and other "tensions"?

F. Topics for debate and forum
1. "No matter what the hidden possibilities may be, the South under the present economy is not capable of attaining the highest economic and cultural development" (p. 22).
2. Education can transform the conflict patterns of the southern people into coöperative patterns.

G. Suggestions for this unit

Notice the warnings on pages 237-239 about the unreliability of crude comparisons. Lynchings are bad and too frequent, but the question is: Are they decreasing and how rapidly over the years? Libraries are good though scarce; are they increasing? Trends and evidences of change or progress need to receive attention.

As you study pages 15-22, paragraphs 38-54, you will note questions and problems relating to resources and leadership; several paragraphs dealing with standards; others referring to agriculture and industry, and still others having to do with various forms of economy and waste. It would probably be good discipline and helpful in viewing the whole if detailed outlining were practiced for these numbered paragraphs in Chapter I for all the remaining units. For example, paragraph 38 emphasizes riches of resources along with poverty of attitude and action; 39 points out the lack of mature leadership; and so on down to 54 which suggests the problem of waste of man and land power.

By using the index to *Southern Regions,* pages 651-664, you can enlarge at will the content of your own knowledge and compose many more questions and topics than those provided under D, E, and F.

NOTES

NOTES

UNIT V

BASIC FACTORS OF REGIONAL EXCELLENCE
AND A
NEW REGIONAL ANALYSIS

THIS UNIT of study will be introductory to more detailed consideration of resources to be set forth in the next two units.

As we scan the paragraphs in pages 22-27, we are invited to appraise, to select, and to understand the excellences and the lags of the southern regions. Land planning and the rebuilding of the agrarian South are viewed as possibilities in the days ahead. For many years the southern states have been falling out of balance with themselves and with the nation. Equilibrium needs to be regained.

The author erects a monumental list of distinctive qualities of the old days that, if re-set in their proper place and proportion, can contribute to the balancing of the South within itself and to the rebuilding of a stronger national whole. The South has been poor, is now poor, has narrowed its ways and still suffers from "culture lag," but as Dr. Odum has many times in many places emphasized with vigor: Growth today and tomorrow, not poverty and lag yesterday, is the fairer measure of a people. What they do with their resources, how they exercise their powers, that is the challenge of the day.

Although the substance of the book is made up largely of maps, tables, charts, graphs, and figures that compare "the South with other regions to the almost uniform discredit of the South," such comparisons should not be given too much weight in a *living*, growing society that avails itself of its potentialities and opportunities.

The southern regions and all other regions of the country exist for more than themselves. To this inescapable fact increased attention must be given. Pages 245 to 290 consider the South in the national picture. The plea for the growth of regional-national integration and for a decrease in the settled contentment with sectional-localism is clear and reasonable. Thinking people as well as experts in government believe that if the nation is to ride evenly and surely through the turbulence of the twentieth century, it must have more unity, balance, equalization, and wholeness than is now possible with forty-eight rafts bumping and colliding with each other, some of them all but sinking, many of them dragging back what ought to be the forward movement of the national ship of state. Hence, in these pages we shall discuss regionalism and sectionalism still further, and shall again look into the six regions, viewing the reasons for their selection and delineation as given in the book.

A. Aims for the student
1. To glimpse comparatively some of the foundation resources and the excellences of the southern regions.
2. To examine the need for movement out of narrow paths of sectionalism into broader ways of regional-national reconstruction and progress.
3. To test and challenge such ideas as "unlimited free competition," "states' rights," "sectionalism," and "national responsibility."
4. To raise the question whether the nation itself can afford to ignore the present condition of disequilibrium between states and regions.

B. Reading material for study
Southern Regions, Chapter I, pp. 22-27; Chapter III, pp. 245-290. (Correction: in the first printing, page 281, the title in the twenty-second line should read *Sections in American History*.)

Suggested additional reading: *The Advancing South*, by Edwin Mims. See also p. 261 in *Southern Regions* for articles in various journals.

C. Definitions and general guidance
Wealth of several kinds is mentioned from time to time. *Human wealth:* abundance of homogeneous people whose worth, ability, and potentiality far outweigh their present poverty. *Natural wealth:* minerals, trees, water, climate, etc. *Artificial wealth:* the result of processing natural wealth and the advancement of industry, commerce, etc. *Capital wealth:* strictly defined would refer to investment in productive equipment while a socio-economic definition might include economic goods and services, as well as money invested, that make for human welfare. A region may have very little money, a very low income, and yet have real wealth. This suggests a fundamental distinction between wealth and prosperity, and also a distinction between private and public wealth or group potentialities and utilization of resources.

Non-liquidity refers to wealth resources that are not easily changed into ready cash. Wealth in land and buildings is not so liquid as wealth in bonds, stocks, and actual money. Broadly speaking, children and youth deprived of good education; land that might be pasturing cattle; artistic and musical ability that might be released—these and many others might be mentioned as intangible non-liquid assets that are bogged down by tradition and inertia.

Value-economy of living; money-economy of spending: Money as a measure of value is so inseparably associated with references to economy that "value-economy" and "money-economy" as terms set apart from each other are somewhat difficult to define. However, from the social and philosophical standpoint "value-economy of living" refers to the more enduring values that belong to sound social institutions; "money-economy of spending," the passing satisfactions enjoyed at the expense of constructive programs of human betterment. Low standards of living may perforce result from injudicious spending. Many southern expenditures may be seen as disproportionately costly against a background of malnourished children and adults, low literacy and educational standards, and shabby housing. (See also definition of *Wages*.)

Institutional services: Hospitals, clinics, schools, libraries, etc.

Culture complex: In addition to the definition of culture in Unit I, if we think of the complexities that cluster around or relate definitely to some aspect of life, this term simplifies itself. Cotton, for example, has long been important in American culture, particularly in southern culture. Around cotton there is a complex of thoughts, attitudes, and acts, historical and contemporary: plantations, Negroes, slavery, war, industry moving south, tenancy and labor problems, employer-employee strife, inventions of new fibres (rayon) and machines (cotton gin and picker), and many near and remote aspects of the cotton "complex." The word "complex" requires an adjective to give it specific meaning, since there are so many uses of the word in anthropology, sociology, psychology, and everyday speech.

Equilibration, equilibrium: A glance at any of the numerous maps and charts showing the great differences between the South and other regions will reveal the out-of-balance condition of the nation. For the best realization of the nation's total cultural equipment, the American people must equilibrate themselves, must bring the states and regions into better balance, into more of an equilibrium. Perfect equipoise is not to be expected, but great wealth and advantage in one area with dire poverty and disadvantage in other areas cannot mean democratic national prosperity.

Romantic realism: Romance in facts as they are. This does not imply contradiction of terms or the fanciful and extravagant, but that facts can be gathered, considered, studied, and presented colorfully; cold facts can be warmed without losing their scientific reliability. Notice the liveliness in paragraphs 60, 61, 62, and 66. The conditions, the realities there discussed are not coldly sketched in black and dull gray but with life and buoyancy. The idea is that the South must so address itself to its many problems and programs. (See question D-2, and definition of *Imaginative exploration*.)

Folkways, stateways: The habits and customs which grow up to meet the needs of the people ripen into *mores* and morals which become the basis of laws, which are forms of stateways. Yet what the people want to do and what they actually do may or may not be in line with what the state or law prescribes. A stateway or law is likely to be respected and enforced when it is actively wanted by the people. An enlightened democracy says: "Children may be educated at public expense; all children must go to school." This law grew out of folk conviction. It is both a stateway and a folkway except where the child-labor folkway is more dominant. A rebellious minority enslaved to an old folkway may resist for a time a progressive stateway even when it has been endorsed by the majority. On the other hand, laws are often flouted when they are out of step with the will or practice of the people, as, for instance, a thirty-mile-an-hour speed limit on an open country road where the actual auto-driving folkway is forty miles an hour. (See definition of *mores* in Unit VII.)

D. Questions primarily on facts and mapograph interpretations
1. In the following maps what differences do you see between the southeastern and southwestern regions? Pages 26, 216, 256 (top half of page), and 260. What do these differences indicate?
2. On page 285, paragraph beginning: "Turning now to the six . . ." illustrate by concrete examples for your region, some of the points set forth.
3. What is the point in the display of forty district maps between pages 262 and 270? Do they indicate a strengthening or a weakening of the importance of the state boundaries? Why do you think so?
4. In his defining of the six regions, how does Dr. Odum come to his conclusions? (Take some such state as Kentucky or Missouri to illustrate your answer.)
5. Give an illustration for each of the five "major storehouses of wealth: natural, technological, artificial, human, and institutional."
6. Of the five major types of resources in the Southeast, wherein is there excellence, and wherein is there deficiency or lag?
7. As you study the excellences recounted in paragraphs 61 and 62, pages 23 and 24, can you see how and why they differ, if they do, from the excellences of the North and West?
8. Can you think of folkways that violate stateways with regard to children, Negroes, Indians, and other aspects of life?

A NEW REGIONAL ANALYSIS

9. How would you illustrate: ". . . seeks more of the value-economy of living and less of the money-economy of spending"?
10. Do you find any cause for optimism about the South of tomorrow? Has the South made any remarkable strides since 1900?

E. Questions primarily on policy and program
1. What did Woodrow Wilson say about sectionalism? Was he right or wrong? Why do you think so?
2. Does paragraph 55, page 22, say: "What was true of the South yesterday and today is not necessarily going to be true of the region tomorrow"? Or does this passage mean something else? If so, what?
3. In paragraph 56, page 22, four points necessary to cultural reconstruction are made. What are they?
4. If we consider "many children," "two races," "long growing season," as three in a list of elemental factors in the cultural and natural equipment of the South, what further factors would you add to the list? Evaluate them as assets or liabilities.
5. Should or should not the national government look upon any disadvantaged people anywhere within the nation's borders (Indian, Negro, poor white) as partly their problem of education? What are your arguments?
6. Granted that for a civilized society to exist on "meat, meal, and molasses"; to encourage child labor in field and factory; and to neglect education, is a sign of abnormality and disintegration, how can remedies for these and other abnormalities be found through "normal processes of reintegration and reconstruction"?
7. What would be the arguments for and against a national proposal and program based upon: "We'll help you to help yourself in proportion as you contribute money and leadership"?

F. Topics for debate and forum
1. Regionalism cannot be attained without change in the American viewpoint. (What is the "American viewpoint"?)
2. If, to educate the children of its disadvantaged areas, a state spreads its money for education (equalization funds) over the entire state for the benefit of all children, the nation should similarly be concerned with the "unequal places" within the national boundaries.
3. Because the quality of many southern people is poor they should be looked upon as a liability rather than as "human wealth."
4. The nation must for its own sake bring about greater equilibrium between states and regions within its borders.
5. On page 263 we read about more than one hundred administrative regions

for various functions. In view of this the importance of state localism must recede more and more in favor of a national-regionalism, if the best interests of *all* the people are to be served.

6. Unlimited free competition means monopoly; monopolies are bad; therefore unlimited free competition must soon be replaced by something better, if civilization is to survive.

NOTES

NOTES

UNIT VI

REGIONS OF NATURAL RICHNESS AND ABUNDANCE
(ORGANIC)

WHEN THE southern regions are compared to other regions of the nation, it is easily seen that they lack much that is found elsewhere and, what is worse, that they have failed to use many things to best advantage even though these things are present in great abundance.

But it is equally true that the southern regions have many resources of better quality and in greater quantity than are to be found elsewhere. The regions with which we are particularly concerned in this study are not poor in natural endowment by any means. Here nature has given advantages and elements which are essential to the prosperity of any region, or any nation. The next two units of this study undertake to make a rough inventory of these natural riches, to show the student some of the potentialities and some of the opportunities of the people of the southern portion of the United States.

Here is abundance of valuable minerals and soils in an exceptionally good climate, a land of great promise to the farmer and the industrialist alike. It would be easy to fan a glowing regional pride into many-tongued flames of exaggerated sectionalism while reading such a listing of resources and a discussion of such nature-given wealth. It is natural and right to be proud of the richness of one's region, whether that region happens to be the South or some other. Such a feeling is the best basis for true patriotism, a valuable asset in any society.

But, before any people allow themselves to be carried away by the pictures of abundance to which they are heirs, it is also well to consider the use they are making of these gifts. Abundance without use means waste. One picture is largely meaningless without the other; both must be seen together if either is to have its full significance. The South has been inclined to magnify the favorable picture of itself and to slight the blemishes of non-use, mis-use, and waste. This is a natural fault, of course, but a fault nevertheless.

The present unit is concerned with the organic resources of the southern regions, the vegetable and animal kingdoms on which men have been primarily dependent in the long history of mankind. The seventh unit will undertake to list and examine the inorganic resources which are being used more and more to replace those which grow. Then will come an account of how we have used and misused these natural gifts. Chapters IV and V of *Southern Regions* are broken into several units for purposes of ease of discussion; it is only when the four units are seen together that the true picture is obtained.

A. Aims for the student
1. To gain a comprehensive, if somewhat rough, view of the abundance of organic resources of the southern regions.
2. In the light of this knowledge to gain some insight into the part this abundance has played in the formation of the culture of the South.
3. To envision to some degree what this abundance might mean to the regions and to the nation under different forms of utilization.

B. Reading material for study
Southern Regions, Chapter I, pp. 27-35; Chapter IV, pp. 291-330.

The student should perhaps be reminded at this point that the suggested additional reading—where there is the time and inclination—can be most satisfactorily accomplished by the topical method. In other words, by using the Tables of Contents and Indexes in these additional books, the thoughts and topics of the main text can be enriched.

Suggested additional reading: *Human Geography of the South,* one or more of Chapters VI through XI. Another valuable book for selected readings is *World Resources and Industries,* by Erich W. Zimmermann.

C. Definitions and general guidance
Demography: This term has its origin in the same root as the word democracy—*demos,* the people. In the literature of social science it has come to be used mostly in connection with studies of population density, distribution, age and sex factors, etc. However, many social scientists feel that this is an unnecessary and perhaps unfortunate contraction of the meaning of the term; that it ought to be wide enough to include all the factors in any social situation which depend primarily on the people concerned. Such a use of the term would include such factors as the customs followed "naturally" and without thought by the folk of a region, their attitudes and sentiments, their ways of "every-day" living. It is in this latter sense that the term is used in this study. Often this use is distinguished from the first by prefixing the word "social."

Agrarian culture: A culture in which the most important element is the

NATURAL RICHNESS AND ABUNDANCE

agricultural, in which transportation and communication, commerce and industry serve the farmer primarily since the farmer controls the greatest portion of the wealth; sets the pattern in social and religious and political thinking and acting. The old plantation South was an agrarian culture; the corn belt region of the present is largely agrarian with a fringe of industrial and commercial cultures which also penetrate it to a large extent. The modern South is perhaps the most distinctly agrarian region in the United States, a truth unconsciously acknowledged in the phrase "King Cotton." (See also definitions of culture and agrarianism.)

Since this unit is largely concerned with factual material, there should be little difficulty in its study. This does not mean, however, that the section is without very important implications for theory and planning. Such an examination of resources illustrates an important part of any regional study, since it forms the essential basis for understanding the area studied. And such understanding, in its turn, is absolutely essential to any workable plan of administration, political or otherwise, to say nothing of reorganization.

D. Questions primarily on facts and mapograph interpretations
 1. What is the average farm size in the United States? In the Southeast? What are the implications of these facts for type of farming, use of machinery, etc.?
 2. What percentage of the nation's timber supply is located in the southeastern region? Is this a regional or national resource? or both? Explain your answer.
 3. What has been the trend of the nursery industry in the region during the past two decades? What is the importance of such an industry, economically and aesthetically, in a regional economy?
 4. Study the charts on page 304. In which basic agricultural products does the southern region lead? In which does it lag? What explanations come to mind readily? What does this situation mean in terms of relation of the southern region to the remainder of the nation?
 5. What is the particular interest of the Southeast in the study of plant and animal life? What are the resources of the region for such study? What is its economic importance?
 6. What are the chief factors in American life making public acquisition of parks and playgrounds of increasing importance? Discuss the resources of the Southeast which might be used in such programs.
 7. What implications arise from the fact that the southeastern region leads the nation in production of cotton and tobacco? Discuss this situation from the point of view of politics, economics, religion, social organization, standards

of living. Can you think of similar impact of other crops or industries in other regions of the nation?

8. The map and table on page 30 show the southeastern region to have the smallest farms, on the average, of any region in the nation. What explanations can you offer for this fact? What is its bearing on the general welfare of the region and of the nation?
9. Study the map, top of page 306. What does this indicate as to the desirable forestry policies of the various regions of the nation?
10. Study the table on page 308, showing where lumber produced in the southern region is consumed. What does this mean in terms of interregional interdependence?
11. Look into some of the recent literature on *chemurgy*. Why should the southern regions be especially interested in this movement?

E. Questions primarily on policy and program

1. Study the figures on page 28 showing the use of the land in the various states and regions. What changes do you think would be beneficial to the southern regions, taking into consideration geographic, economic and social factors as they now exist?
2. Discuss possible and feasible plans whereby the utilization of food supplied by nature in the waterways of the region might be combined with a recreational program.
3. Given soil and climate highly favorable to the growth of timber, how can this resource be better utilized?
4. What is the southern interest in the growth of the rayon industry? Does the growth of this industry conflict with the general welfare of the region? of the nation? How?
5. Compare the ease of access of parks and forests in the southern mountains to those in the western mountains, in relation to centers of population. What does this indicate as to relative value in use?
6. Can the recent preachments of diversification and "live-at-home" programs be reconciled with the economic theory that each region should specialize in the product which it can produce at best advantage and buy from others what is produced only at extra cost? How does this apply to the southeastern region? to other regions of the nation?

F. Topics for debate and forum

1. What the South and the nation as a whole need is the utilization of the vast quantities of land now lying idle. (This might be stated also as: What is needed is more intensive cultivation of a smaller proportion of the nation's or region's land resources.)

NATURAL RICHNESS AND ABUNDANCE

2. The small farms of the Southeast, occupied largely by owners, form a valuable bulwark against the encroachment of radical political and social theories, and should be preserved because of this function.
3. Cotton is a national necessity as a source of cheap clothing; hence, the cotton industry should be protected by a national tax which is collected from all regions.
4. The State of North Carolina pays into the national treasury internal revenue taxes far above its proportion of population or wealth. These funds should be expended in the state from which they are paid, or at least within the region. (It is suggested that figures on payment of taxes and expenditures of federal funds by various states and regions be investigated before this statement is discussed.)
5. An eminent social scientist more or less facetiously remarked recently that several areas, including most of the Southeast, were not needed for agricultural use and should be turned over "to the foxes and briars." From the national point of view, list all the arguments you can think of for and against this position.
6. The Southeast's land has been over-estimated as to its quality; and besides, it is more susceptible to erosion than other areas.

G. Suggestions for this unit

Several of the questions carry the student beyond the material actually presented in the sections assigned. This is done with the purpose of emphasizing the social implications of the factual materials, on the theory that facts derive most of their importance from their social meanings. Use of the index to *Southern Regions* and other works cited, especially *Human Geography of the South,* will be found most useful in this connection.

NOTES

NOTES

UNIT VII

REGIONS OF NATURAL RICHNESS AND ABUNDANCE (INORGANIC)

Modern civilization is distinguished from the older civilizations as those of Egypt, Greece, and Rome, as well as from the social organizations of the so-called primitive peoples largely by our much greater dependence upon inorganic materials. For countless centuries man knew how to use only his own strength and those inorganic resources such as sticks and stones, soils and streams, which met his needs with very little change from the condition in which nature supplied them.

Gradually—very gradually until recently—man developed ways of changing the natural ores into metals, of obtaining power from coal or flowing water, of devising mechanical forms not found in nature which enabled him to move natural objects and products over great distances. The recency of this development is illustrated by the fact that even so late as the Civil War fuel for transforming iron ore into metal was derived in some parts of the United States from wood reduced to charcoal and then used in smelting.

The development of industries, manufactures, and the like (technology) is not the concern of this unit of study; but it should be held in mind, since the inorganic resources of a region are valuable to a great extent because we have worked out means of using them rather than because of their mere presence. For a people having the skills and techniques, the presence or absence of such resources immediately becomes of the greatest importance in their regional economy.

Soil and sunshine, rainfall and rivers are inorganic resources of a type which are so closely tied up with the growth of crops and forests and beasts and fishes that they easily point to the close connection between the organic and inorganic resources. A little more imagination is needed to see the connection between coal and the school system, or oil and regional economic dependence; but reflection will show that these basic sources of power and their control have a very real and very important effect on our entire social organization. They enable us to do things we could not do otherwise, and how we use the power we derive from them is in part a measure of the success of our civilization.

For these reasons, a survey of the inanimate resources of a region is an essential first step to an understanding of the regional culture. Further, prediction or control of the future of that regional culture will also be dependent upon the accuracy of such a survey.

In the sections of the study assigned for this unit the store of inorganic resources in the regions is discussed. Throughout the study the limitations imposed by lack of these materials, and the possibilities opened up by their presence can be seen always, sometimes dimly, sometimes vividly, as a background against which the pictures of the cultural development are thrown in relief.

A. **Aims for the student**
   1. To acquire a generalized knowledge of the inorganic resources of the southern regions.
   2. To glimpse some of the possibilities this abundance of material wealth opens up to the southern regions, and, through them, to the nation and to the world.
   3. To learn something of the trend in the use of such resources in the southern regions as compared with other portions of the nation.

B. **Reading material for study**
   Southern Regions, Chapter I, pp. 35-39; Chapter IV (review pp. 275-290), pp. 290-330.

   Suggested additional reading: *Human Geography of the South*, Chapters V, XII, and XIII.

C. **Definitions and general guidance**
   Mores: The Latin word *"mores"* (singular: *mos*) is about equivalent to our word "standards." The *mores* hold a high place of morality or rightness; they resist change and are not to be questioned; they connect vitally with the welfare of the people. The Christian religion and monogamy, for example, are among the *mores* of our western world. (See definition of *Folkways* in Unit V.)

   Natural Resources: A natural resource is something which can be used by a given society and which is supplied by nature. Thus coal and iron, rainfall and sunshine, are natural resources in our society. But neither coal nor iron were natural resources for the Indians who occupied this continent three hundred years ago, since Indians had no means of using either. This idea of the value of a "natural resource" depending upon our ability to use it is important. Inventions are constantly bringing into being new resources,

NATURAL RICHNESS AND ABUNDANCE

as new ways of using hitherto unused substances are created. Further invention increases the value of the now recognized natural resources by developing more efficient means of using them. Thus, natural resources cannot be separated from invention and technology.

Optimum realization: The close connection between technology and natural resources is discussed more fully in the next assignment. But Dr. Odum rightly calls this connection to the mind of the student in his discussion of natural resources by speaking of optimum realization, which means the best possible combination of resources and skills for their use. This best possible combination varies constantly, of course, with the discovery of new sources of materials and the changes in techniques constantly being made by engineers.

Superabundance: By this term is meant merely that there are more materials supplied by nature than we are now able to use under conditions of optimum realization; not more materials than we can use, now or later.

Imaginative exploration: Many persons think of science as being entirely cold-blooded and matter of fact, interested only in charts and figures. This is far from being true, of the best scientists at least. It is the people with imagination enough to see implications of facts and figures, maps and charts, who make the worthwhile contributions to human life. Imagination is required for the best possible use of these tools, just as the architect must be able to see the great cathedral in the "sticks and stones" from which it is to be built. Similarly, the student is expected to use a healthy imagination in interpreting the significance of the facts and figures pertaining to the natural resources of the region he studies.

The above definitions should be kept in mind while the assignment is worked out, since they give something of the spirit in which it is believed the study should be undertaken. Other definitions of specific resource items may be found readily in any good dictionary.

The student should always strive to keep in mind the close connection between inorganic resources, such as soils and climate, and organic resources, such as plants and animals; and the more important connection between these resources and the social organization of the region resting upon them.

D. Questions primarily on facts and mapograph interpretations

1. What is the situation of the southeastern region as to coal resources? in quantity, quality, and amount used today?
2. Why is the production of phosphate of peculiar importance to the southeastern region?
3. What percentage of the nation's supply of petroleum products originates in

the southern regions? About what percentage of these products is used in these regions? What does this mean in terms of inter-regional relations?
4. Approximately what percentage of the nation's iron is produced in the southeastern region? Why is regional production of iron particularly important?
5. Discuss the relative importance of abundant supplies of suitable building materials in our southern resources.
6. The active principle in "anti-knock" gasoline is extracted from sea water. Many other minerals are present in the sea and might be extracted, it is known. What does this imply as to the potential wealth of the southeastern region?
7. Compare the list of minerals on page 318 with the table of mineral wealth produced on page 320. From this comparison discuss the relation between natural resources and their use.
8. Study the maps on pages 212 and 296. Discuss the general relation between heavy rainfall and population density. How do you account for the higher population density in some regions of lower rainfall?
9. What explanation of the high percentage of developed water power in the Southeast do you find in the map of rainfall and the number of clear days from the map and chart on page 296?
10. What is the connection between the long growing season in the Southeast and the agricultural situation, as to crops grown? as to retention of natural fertility? as to erosion?
11. What has been the effect of a superabundance of navigable streams on the social and economic development of the southeastern region?
12. What are the implications of the maps on page 300 as to a one-crop system of agriculture?
13. Apply the map on page 306, showing a "natural" condition to a discussion of land use in forestry and agriculture and the preservation of soils. What does this mean as to the influence of natural conditions on cultural uses?
14. Why do you suppose *Southern Regions* places highways, railways, and waterways "between the realm of natural endowment and technological efficiency"?

E. Questions primarily on policy and program
1. It is argued that the great abundance of rainfall and sunshine in the southeastern region is a serious liability as well as a powerful asset. Examine these two ideas critically. Then outline a plan, roughly, whereby you believe that these factors might be used to better advantage.
2. What is the connection between population density and developed water power in the various regions of the nation? What does this situation indicate as to the relation between natural forces and the cultural, man-made situation?
3. Discuss practical means by which the supplies of building stone, shown on map on page 326, might result in better living conditions for the people of

NATURAL RICHNESS AND ABUNDANCE

the various regions. What is the implication of the charts on page 328 for such a program?

4. From the maps on pages 322 and 324, discuss the industrial future of the southern regions. What public or private policies do you think would insure a better use of these sources of energy? What are the available resources to which this energy might profitably be applied?
5. Recently the Department of Commerce issued warnings to aviators not to fly over a huge gas field in Texas, since the vast quantity of gas escaping into the air might be ignited by the exhaust from their motors. Discuss this situation from the point of view of public and private property.
6. Discuss beautiful and inspiring scenery as a "natural resource."

F. Topics for debate and forum

1. Resolved: that the traditional right of a person to exploit his land property as he sees fit be limited in certain cases. (Petroleum and gas, for example, may be drained from below the surface of one tract of land through a well drilled on another tract.)
2. No person has a right to allow his soil to be destroyed through wasteful methods of agriculture. (What of the interest of the river navigator in a system of agriculture which allows excessive erosion and thereby destroys his opportunity to continue his business?)
3. The many waterways of the southern regions provide a potential means of cheap transportation for heavy freight which should be developed and maintained.
4. The southeastern region is really fortunate in that many of its natural resources are undeveloped since they might have been wasted had development begun at an earlier time.

64 NOTES

NOTES

GENERAL DISTRIBUTION OF EROSION, 1933
Adapted from the U. S. Bureau of Agricultural Economics

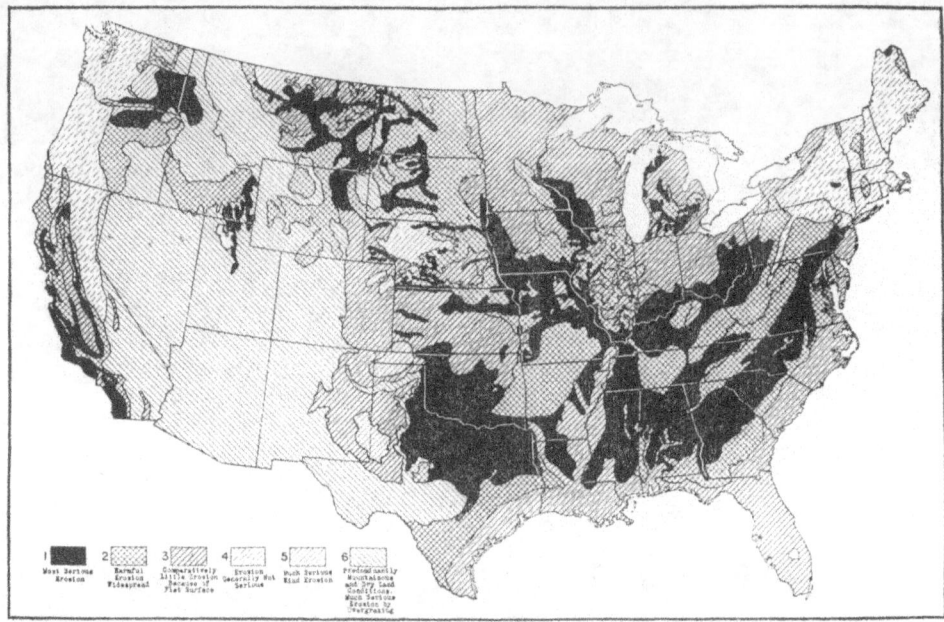

A distinguished anthropogeographer returning to the Southeast recently wrote as follows: "I must say that the cotton Piedmont is a lot farther gone than I had expected. The problem appears to me to be perfectly staggering. The erosive qualities of the greater part of the soils appear much lower than anticipated. That is, I think the popular theme that these southern uplands are peculiarly sensitive to wash is a myth. On the other hand, their abuse is well-nigh incredible under the cotton economy, and the necessary breaking of that socio-economic pattern if the country is not ultimately to be left to the foxes and briars is about as tough a task of regeneration as one can imagine."

PRELIMINARY ESTIMATE OF SOIL IMPOVERISHMENT AND DESTRUCTION BY EROSION
(Areas in Acres)

REGION	Approximate Area of Region	Severely Impoverished or Soil Washed off	Devastated	Total Erosion	Per Cent
Piedmont	46,000,000	12,000,000	4,500,000	16,500,000	35.8
Triassic Piedmont	5,000,000	1,200,000	400,000	1,600,000	32.0
Appalachian Mountains	78,000,000	12,000,000	3,000,000	15,000,000	19.2
Mississippi-Alabama-Georgia Sandy Lands	27,000,000	6,500,000	2,000,000	8,500,000	31.4
Southern Brown Loam	17,000,000	4,500,000	1,800,000	6,300,000	37.0
Texas-Arkansas-Louisiana Sandy Lands	33,000,000	9,500,000	1,500,000	11,000,000	33.3
Texas-Alabama-Mississippi Black Belt	12,000,000	4,500,000	1,000,000	5,500,000	45.8
Red Plains of Texas, Oklahoma	36,000,000	15,000,000	3,000,000	18,000,000	50.0
Total	254,000,000	65,200,000	17,200,000	82,400,000	32.4
Estimates of other southern areas, e. g., Ozarks, coastal plain*		10,000,000	5,000,000	15,000,000	....
Grand Total, South	254,000,000	75,200,000	22,200,000	97,400,000	....
Total for Nation		125,000,000	34,200,000	159,200,000	....
Per Cent which South is of Total					61.1

*The above table except the estimates in this line adapted from H. H. Bennett, *American Geographic Review*, May, 1933.
Reprinted from page 38 in *Southern Regions*.

UNIT VIII

REGIONAL TECHNOLOGY, DEFICIENCY AND WASTE
(LAND)

Is THERE any relation between the soul of a people and the soil upon which they move and have their being? Whether there is or not, it can be said that the spirit of a people need not dwell in the lowlands of self-pity and inaction because of hard and wasteful days and ways. The best cure for self-pity is constructive activity. If today the Aran Islanders off the coast of Ireland can literally make their soil by hammering rock to powder, by toting heavy loads of seaweed up the towering cliffs, by utilizing every crumb of soil and rocky crevice in order to grow their vegetable food, then surely the people of a land still possessed of clay and sand and topsoil can gird themselves to fill the gullies and build the needed terraces, to stop the evil waste before it is too late, to plant upward-pointing trees and crops, and in so doing build up their spirit and morale.

The section dealing with southern inadequacy of science, invention, skills, management, and organization with their resultant deficiency and waste presents a distressing picture of the misuse of land and other natural resources over a comparatively long period of time. It is fairly clear that if the present conditions continue to dominate the scene, tragic consequences are in store for the people of the southeastern region.

Soil once washed away cannot quickly be restored. Gullies that are the inevitable consequences of a rapidly eroding soil render vast areas unfit for the production of any type of crop, tree, or pasture. It is unthinkable that any self-respecting people, who themselves will never see the muddy rivers run clear, should say, "What do we care? Let posterity make the best of it." Future leadership in the South, in spite of all the fine things that may be done immediately, will have to face the ultimate results of twentieth century failure to plan early enough for the future. The general predicament of the rural Southeast, the numerical growth of farm tenancy, the increasing exhaustion of soil productivity through erosion and single-crop practices, and other glaring evidences of deficiency and waste bring out the question: What has the future in store for the South unless drastic steps are taken at once to correct the malpractices?

This and the next several units emphasize from various angles the conditions and prospects of land and people, of agriculture and industry, of poverty and wealth.

A. **Aims for the student**
   1. To visualize the land problem as it confronts the southeasterner on every hand.
   2. To foster constructive resolutions and to promote definite plans and activities.
   3. To promote in local areas some concerted plans for the correction of difficulties.
   4. To coördinate all local activities into the single aim of achieving a better livelihood for the people of the South.

B. **Reading material for study**
   Southern Regions, Chapter I, pp. 39-47; Chapter V, pp. 331-374.

   Suggested additional reading: *The Wasted Land*, by Gerald Johnson. One of our leading American journalists weaves the main threads of *Southern Regions* into a simplified fabric in his own clear style that is both interesting and informative.

C. **Definitions and general guidance**
   Chemurgic: Putting science, and chemistry in particular, to work. Many crops can themselves be thus improved, and many, such as cotton, corn, and soy beans, can be transformed into various commodities other than food. While the so-called "farm chemurgic" (through the Farm Chemurgic Council and the Chemical Foundation, Inc.) emphasizes soil and the farmer, it seems inevitable that the manufacturer and the general public will profit from the new products.
   Coöperative purchasing: A plan whereby any group buys in large quantities through a purchasing agent on a non-profit basis.
   Coöperative selling: A plan whereby any group sells products through a central agency rather than individually.
   Legumes: Plants, commonly the pod-bearing crops such as black-eyed peas, soy beans, and others that take nitrogen from the air and fix it in the soil by means of nodules on their roots.
   One-crop system: The practice by farmers of planting one type of crop, such as cotton, year after year on the same piece of ground. Cotton, corn, and tobacco all impoverish the soil as compared with legumes that benefit the soil.

D. **Questions primarily on facts and mapograph interpretations**
   1. What proportion of the tillable soil in the Southeast consists of eroded lands? Compare with the rest of the United States.

2. In what ways do erosion and other forms of waste of natural resources affect adversely standards of living of southeastern farmers?
3. Compare the Southeast with other areas as to the number of pure-bred cattle. What need is indicated?
4. Compare the Southeast with other areas as to farm implements and conveniences. Should every farm have a tractor? Why?
5. How does the Southeast compare with other sections in the use of commercial fertilizers? Why should so much fertilizer be needed?
6. Contrast the condition of homes and the supply of lumber in the Southeast. If the book had had a table on the consumption of house paint, where would the South be found?
7. Summarize twelve items in which the Southeast lags behind other areas. How many of these lags could be overcome within a generation?
8. From what areas does the Southeast receive Christmas trees, spinach, carrots, cabbages, milk, and cheese? Why are these not supplied locally?
9. Is farming a seasonal or a year-round job? What can farmers do during the winter months? If you live on a farm make a list of the specific things you could do profitably during the winter months which would tend to improve the farm.
10. Compare the Southeast with Minnesota in coöperative buying and selling. Why the difference?
11. How does the South rank with other regions with respect to the manufacture of textiles and cigarettes? Is there any connection here with the one-crop system of the South?
12. Contrast interest rates in the South with those in other areas. How do you account for the difference?
13. Point out dangers inherent in the growth of row crops in an area with an abundant rainfall as in the Southeast.
14. Point out the dangers to soil fertility of bottom lands caused by eroded hillsides.
15. How can the second sentence of paragraph 96, page 47, be explained?

E. Questions primarily on policy and program
   1. What substitutions may be made in order to save southeastern farmers the financial losses involved in the purchase of excessive amounts of commercial fertilizer?
   2. In what ways may topography help to determine the amount of farm machinery needed or advisable for an area?
   3. Why are deficiencies in coöperatives related to illiteracy and lower standards of living?
   4. Account for the comparative progress the Southeast has made with respect

to highway improvement. What would the building of more hard-surfaced highways mean for the South? for the nation?
5. Account for the inability of the South to develop production along all lines for which there is a local or regional demand.

F. Topics for debate and forum
1. The Civil War retarded the South to such an extent that it is lagging behind the rest of the country in most respects. If given time, the slack will be taken up.
2. Southern people are materially minded, else they would have improved their various institutions before spending so much on roads and automobiles.
3. The rainfall of the Southeast is so heavy that soil erosion cannot be avoided. (How is frost related to soil erosion?)
4. Coöperative purchasing and selling cannot hope to succeed as a permanent practice because of difficulties of management.

G. Suggestions for this unit

It is suggested as a point of practical departure that the student make a careful analysis of land use in his home community. In this analysis special care should be paid to pointing out ways in which the land has been robbed of its fertility through poor crop practices and through erosion.

A further part of the analysis should be concerned with ways and means of restoring to the soil some of its original depth and fertility. The student should study carefully the steps that may be taken in effecting control of rainflow in the areas affected. It is suggested, further, that a comprehensive and detailed sketch map be made which would indicate the particular steps that may be taken in the restoration of soil fertility and in stopping soil erosion.

NOTES

NOTES

NOTES

Regional Distribution of Tonnage and Expenditures for Bought Fertilizer, 1929

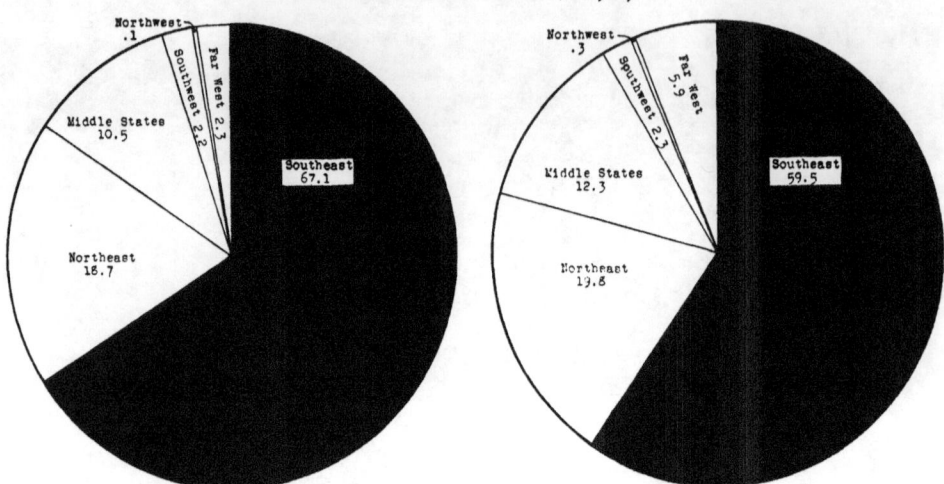

Regional Distribution of the Total Tons of Commercial Fertilizer Bought in the United States During the Crop Year of 1929

Regional Distribution of the Total Expenditure by United States Farmers for All Types of Bought Fertilizers During the Crop Year of 1929

Regional Importance of Expenditures for Fertilizers, Feed and Labor, 1929

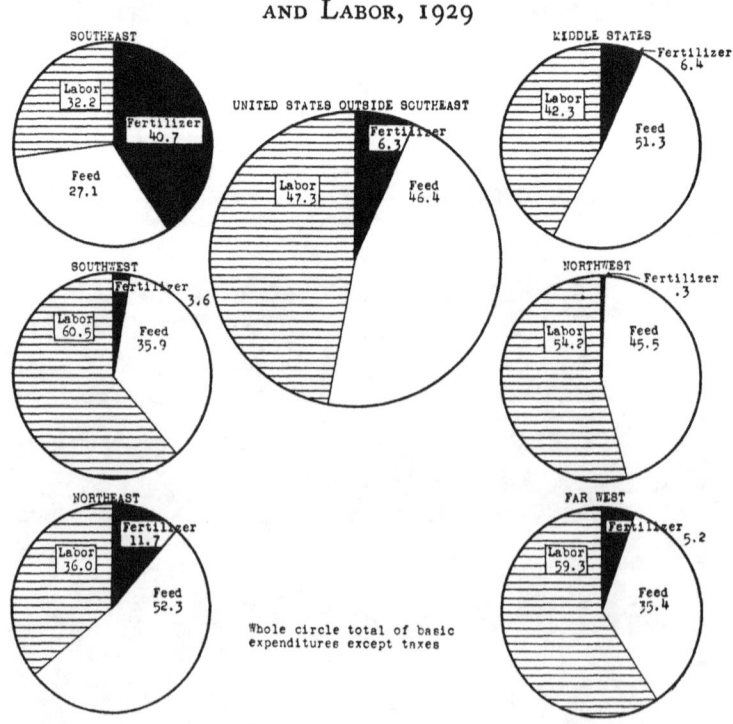

Whole circle total of basic expenditures except taxes

Reprinted from page 40 in *Southern Regions*.

UNIT IX

REGIONAL TECHNOLOGY, DEFICIENCY AND WASTE
(MAN)

THE NATURAL resources of the Southeast afford enough quantity and quality in men and materials for the area to become practically self-supporting. The relative mildness of the climate, the abundant rainfall, the topographic features from seacoast to piedmont and mountain afford abundant waterfall for the development of diversified industry which, if associated with a varied agriculture and supported by an educated public, should make of the Southeast one of the most desirable areas for the development of a great culture. The technological lag manifested in the absence of diversified industry, in the relatively lower wages paid the industrial workers in the South, in the lack of invested capital and in the adverse interest rates available, are difficulties which need not exist always. At present the retardation of the South in these particulars is more relative than absolute.

The strides the South has made in textile and tobacco manufacturing in competition with other areas is an example of achievement that is possible along other industrial lines. In the field of textiles, for example, it is a far cry from the present supremacy of the Carolinas in yarn manufacturing to the day following the close of the Civil War when an evangelist, revivalizing the town of Salisbury and observing the desperate condition of the town's poor whites, said: "Next to religion Salisbury needs a cotton mill." The South's meager beginnings in the textile industry, generated through impulses similar to the experience in Salisbury; the overcoming of practical odds; the building of a great industry in the face of what the experts said was certain defeat because the South could not hope to compete with New England in the manufacture of cotton goods, is an example of the type of leadership and perseverance that is needed to establish the Southeast on a firmer manufacturing basis in all lines of industry. The Southeast has a practically unlimited resource in the abundance of a native-born, homogeneous labor force with which to man its industries. The labor force is one of the greatest assets a region can possess in establishing itself in any major line of industry.

Land and the farmer, industry and the worker will be studied still further in Units X-XIII.

A. Aims for the student

1. To measure the present southern levels of health and wealth with a view to higher accomplishment in farm and factory.
2. To make clearer by comparison with other regions the extent of southern lags and deficiencies in agriculture and industry.
3. To suggest some changes that will mean the replacement of waste by efficiency and economy.

B. Reading material for study

Southern Regions, Chapter I, pp. 49-55; Chapter V, pp. 331-374.

Suggested additional reading: *Preface to Peasantry,* by Arthur F. Raper, Chapters VI, VII, VIII, IX.

C. Definitions and general guidance

Through a consideration of the material in this section the student should be able to get a direct comparison between the various social and economic resources of the Southeast and of other parts of the country.

Tangible wealth as used in the chart on page 48 refers to the recorded or book value of all property owned by all the people in a state. When this total value is divided by the number of persons in the state the per capita wealth is secured.

Income refers to the total amount of funds received, through wages or interest or both, during a stated period of time.

Wages: Money wages are the income received from work. Real wages must be thought of in terms of purchasing power. A man may receive the same money wage year after year; but, if during that time the cost of living goes higher, his real wages are correspondingly lowered.

D. Questions primarily on facts and mapograph interpretations

1. Compare the Southeast with other areas with respect to manufacturing industries. Explain the differences between the regions.
2. From the maps on pages 342, 344, 346, and 348, indicate a dozen aspects of southern life that might be remedied within the next ten years.
3. Compare wages and income paid in the Southeast with wages and income in other areas. How can differences be explained?
4. Why should there be a "flow of talent" out of the Southeast? What is its extent?
5. How do the maps on page 370 reflect the health and wealth conditions of the several regions?
6. To what extent is the lag observed in the Southeast "rural" rather than regional or sectional?

TECHNOLOGY, DEFICIENCY AND WASTE

7. What can be pointed out on pages 338 and 339 that challenges the Southeast to new efforts in producing and marketing fruits and vegetables?
8. Is there any indication in the map on page 336 (bottom) that the Southeast could use more electric power? Explain.
9. List the fundamental factors in production to be used as an index of measurement according to Stuart Chase. How does the South compare with other areas on this basis?
10. Compare the Southeast with other areas as to all animal units—cattle, sheep and lambs, swine, and chickens.
11. What evidence can be found that the South needs to change its ways with regard to pure-bred cattle? Why emphasize "pure-bred"?

E. **Questions primarily on policy and program**
1. What steps can be taken to stop the trend toward large scale mechanical farming and the consequent trend toward peasantry in the Southeast?
2. A political "boss" in Tennessee has threatened to have a law passed in the Tennessee legislature that would forbid the use of the Rust cotton picker on Tennessee farms. Indicate why such a law, if enacted, would hurt more than it would help?
3. What would be the effects on the Southeast of a sudden widespread use of perfected cotton pickers in the Southwest?
4. Before the lag in industry in the Southeast can be corrected, what fundamental changes in education and politics must take place?
5. Give reasons for the relatively lower wages paid in industry in the Southeast as compared with other regions.
6. To what extent are the lack of industrial development, lower wages, and smaller capital investments in the South due to the same conditions?

F. **Topics for debate and forum**
1. Wages should be lower in the South because the cost of living is lower.
2. The landlord "skins" the tenant; the tenant "skins" the land.
3. The continued "flow of talent" over a long period of time has left the South's population today intellectually inferior to the population of other sections.
4. The relative immobility of the population of the South has produced a "stagnated" condition that has caused the South to drop behind other areas in progress and in achievement.
5. The Southeast can never hope to overtake other sections of the country with respect to technological improvements along all lines. The Southeast should "live its own life" and forget about comparisons with other parts of the country. After all, the Southeast is "different."
6. The backwardness of the Southeast is due to a superabundance of natural resources. People in the Southeast have had an "easy existence."

NOTES

NOTES

NOTES

UNIT X

AN AGRARIAN COUNTRY

WHETHER WE look upon the South of the past or present it is an agrarian[1] country. Its future will be measured by the achievements of its farms and farm people. So much attention has been focused upon the traditions and romance of the plantation life of the "Old South" that little thought has been given to the great number of small farms that were tilled by thousands of whites without the aid of slaves. It is likely that few have realized the continuing division of plantations into small farms from the 1860's to the present. However, the maps on pages 380 and 384 will show the South to be a region of numerous small farms—"In the Southeast there are more than five and a quarter million farms; in the Southwest nearly another million; and in the two about half of the farms and farm folk in the nation." Is peasantry just ahead?

One of the nation's early leaders who lived in the South had an agrarian ideal for America. He hoped that this nation would always remain a democracy of landholders who would produce enough food and clothing for a simple peaceful life undisturbed by the complexity, competitions, and inequalities of city life. He hoped that manufacturing would be kept in Europe always. The South followed this colonial pattern for a long time, and there are those who would have it free from twentieth century industrial contamination.

Thus, the South has raised things which it could sell to regions or nations engaged in manufacture, and has had to buy finished products outside of its borders. It has come to put a major emphasis upon cash crops in order to get funds with which to buy tools, fertilizer, clothing, and other machine products. This has led to a shortage of agricultural products needed for home consumption, and it has so exhausted the soil that fertilizer has to be used in excessive quantities.

The South is truly an agrarian country, but it must reorganize its crop production and balance this with industry or become a permanent colonial-type of exploited peasant country.

[1] This chapter does not assume any pure agrarianism that wants no industry, but recognizes rather the dominant agricultural increment in the total culture.

A. Aims for the student

1. To recognize the predominance of an agrarian economy in the South, together with the major deficiencies of this economy.
2. To develop an understanding of the methods of analysis which are necessary to planning for optimum production in each subregion.
3. To recognize the need for reorganization of agriculture and to realize the promise of an abundant life which reorganization will yield.
4. To stimulate students to seek the discovery of undeveloped and underdeveloped resources in their own localities.

B. Reading material for study

Southern Regions, Chapter I, pp. 55-69; Chapter VI, pp. 375-430. When a number of maps are examined one after another they build up a picture or tell a story. Here are twenty-two maps arranged in such a way that you get a picture of the South as an agrarian country. Before reading anything in connection with this unit examine the list of maps in the order given. Then write down what the maps tell you: use pp. 56; 238; 30; 380; 60; 412; 486; 254; 12; 42; 336; 342; 196; 396; 346; 348; 38; 66; 418; 44; 402; 20.

Suggested additional reading: *Culture in the South*, Chapters IV and XVI. Also, *Agrarianism*, by T. J. Cauley.

C. Definitions and general guidance

Agrarianism may be defined simply as a culture organized around the processes of raising plants and animals. However, the term is sometimes used controversially to mean on the one hand a nearly self-sufficient culture which minimizes or excludes any separate organization of life around machine production (industrialism); and on the other, to mean a balancing of these two organizations of life activities so as to realize an optimum supply of all goods.

Colonial economy: The production primarily of raw products in one region or country to be exchanged for goods manufactured in another.

Tenancy: A system of farming by which non-owners till the soil and harvest crops in exchange for the subsistence provided by owners of the land.

Lag: The persistence of a system or practice after related systems or practices have changed or been abandoned. (See Unit III.)

Cash crop: A crop raised primarily to secure cash, and not directly for food, shelter, or clothing. Cotton and tobacco are crops which must be sold by the farmer for cash or exchanged for goods if value is to be derived from them.

Mobility: The physical movement of people from place to place is fre-

AN AGRARIAN COUNTRY

quently referred to as spatial or horizontal mobility. When people change their social or economic position, vertical mobility. Then there is mobility of ideas also, when, by learning and communication, people change their position of mind or viewpoint.

D. **Questions primarily on facts and mapograph interpretations**
   1. Why is the South called an "Agrarian Country"? How much of the area is rural, and what proportion of the people are devoted to rural interests? How does the percentage of income from agriculture compare with the amount from this source throughout the nation?
   2. How many farms are there in the South, and what is their average size? Are they tending to get smaller or larger? How do you explain these facts, and why are they important?
   3. How much of the world's supply of cotton is raised in the South? In what southern states does the raising of this crop predominate? How many farm families are engaged in producing it?
   4. Do most of the people in the richest cotton lands own their farms? How do home ownership and tenancy in the South compare with other regions of the country? In which states is tenancy greatest? Is it increasing or decreasing? (See pp. 61, 391, 412, 418, 486, 254, 12.)
   5. Give and explain seven reasons for expecting a continually smaller amount of cotton to be produced in the future. What is meant by the need for a substitute economy?
   6. After cotton what crop is produced in greatest relative abundance in the South? Give the relative production of other principal crops grown successfully in the region.
   7. What products necessary to a rich general agriculture are notably lacking in many states of the South and how does this affect the soil, diet, and income of the region? (See pp. 394-396, and maps on pp. 396, 66, 348, 38.)
   8. Are the crops raised in a certain locality the only ones that *will* grow well, or is this largely a matter of custom? Prove your conclusion by showing what crops are raised and what crops can be raised in a certain area. What crops that now receive little attention would grow well in the locality in which you live?
   9. How many of the major crops can be grown in the South? Which ones could be increasingly raised with profit and which ones decreased with advantage?
   10. Does present consumption furnish a measure of the amount of production that is needed? What are some of the foods needed by the South that it does not produce in sufficient (optimum) quantity?
   11. Compare Tennessee subregions with adjoining ones in Georgia and Alabama;

and explain the changes which might be expected to decrease erosion, increase yields, and raise standards of living.

E. **Questions primarily on policy and program**
   1. State two or three interpretations of an agrarian ideal. Which of these seems to you both desirable and possible of realization?
   2. What does the author mean by "dilemmas of agriculture" and "the need for reconstruction of agriculture"?
   3. Interpret and give reasons for accepting or rejecting the statement: "There cannot be a successful national agriculture in which all the farming regions produce all the necessities of their economic lives, disregarding the comparative advantages of certain regional specializations."
   4. What are some of the major factors which should be considered in determining the crop specialization of a locality or subregion?
   5. Locate the "Uplands" of the mid-South and show how relations to other regions must be studied in order to judge what agricultural products should be planned for this sub-area. What seems to be the most promising program?
   6. What deficiencies stand in the way of a more abundant life in the South?
   7. What has been the "subsequent influence on the tenant system" of the "spell of the old plantation economy"?

F. **Topics for debate and forum**
   1. Democracy wobbles as one region has so-called overproduction of foodstuff while another region suffers from actual underconsumption.
   2. The South is naturally agrarian; therefore, further industrialization of the region should be discouraged.
   3. City life and urban industry can be combined happily with agrarian pursuits in the South.

NOTES

NOTES

UNIT XI

MEASURES OF INDUSTRY AND WEALTH

The picture of the Agrarian South is one of unfulfilled promise. At present the scene is one of widespread and increasing tenancy, land erosion and exhaustion, extreme emphasis on cash crops, shortage of pasture lands and farm animals. It appears that crops are not always produced according to the profits they will yield nor the need people have for them, and not even because they are best suited to soil and climate; but rather because of custom and leadership in the past. It is inevitable that production of one of the principal crops, cotton, will decline. For this reason there must be some rearrangement of the farming habits of the people. If the people can be awakened to their need for more dairy products, poultry products, small fruits, and many other things which will improve their diet and enjoyment of life, the reorganization of agriculture will gradually be achieved. Something must be done to save the soils from exhaustion and washing away.

But it has been emphasized that a purely agrarian culture tends to develop a colonial pattern wherein manufactured goods must be bought from other regions or nations. Since the South has followed this pattern of life during much of its history, it is clear that the region will never reach its full possibility for abundant living without developing its industrial resources to a proper balance with agriculture. "The Southeast being a heavily loaded debtor region faces an unusually adverse trade balance. It not only does not have adequate opportunity for earning, but its money, hard earned, flows out and out to enrich other regions, often contrary to its economic advantages and diminishing the income and purchasing power of the people. The remedying of this situation is the objective of . . . planning for industrial development."

A. Aims for the student
1. To discover the nature and extent of the South's present industrial development, and recognize the accompanying urban trend.
2. To learn regional wealth-poverty indices and by applying them to the major regions get a comparative rating of southern wealth and industry.
3. To recognize the principal reasons for the present status of southern industry.

88 MANUAL FOR SOUTHERN REGIONS

  4. To analyze the undeveloped industrial resources of the South and examine the factors which must guide industrial expansion.

B. **Reading material for study**
Southern Regions, Chapter I, pp. 69-81; Chapter V, pp. 351-355; Chapter VII, pp. 431-441. Incidental readings: pp. 17, 199, 221, and 405.

Suggested additional reading: *Culture in the South,* Chapters V and VI. Also, *The Collapse of Cotton Tenancy,* by C. S. Johnson, E. R. Embree, and W. W. Alexander—a strong little book of some seventy pages.

C. **Definitions and general guidance**
Urbanization: The process of town and city growth. Many people are leaving the dwellings scattered through the open country and are moving to the industrial towns or cities.

Decentralization of industry: This term has several meanings: (a) Regionally it refers to the movement of industry from large crowded areas to those of less congestion as, for example, the movement of the textile mills from crowded New England to the South; (b) from the community standpoint, the movement of industry to the outer fringe of towns and cities, as illustrated in the small industries of English planned towns; (c) the location of separate industrial processes or part manufacture in scattered communities or towns rather than to have every detail of work done in one central location, as in the case of certain automobile manufacturing.

Naval stores: Such resinous products as pitch, tar, and turpentine.

Technology, technological: Systematic, applied knowledge connected with industrial development. The science in bridge-building comes from mathematics, physics, and chemistry; the actual building is done through engineering technology. An extension of the word is used to denote skills and mastery in social control, as social technology.

D. **Questions primarily on facts and mapograph interpretations**
  1. Are people going from the farms to the cities of the South in great numbers? What states are actually decreasing in rural population? How many people of the South are now engaged in agriculture and how many in manufacturing?
  2. What are the few major industries, and in which, if any, does the South lead?
  3. What percentage of the supply of paper pulp does the South furnish? What portion of the pulp mills are located in the region, and what percentage of paper manufacture goes on in the South?
  4. The South has half of the lumber mills in the country and has half of the

INDUSTRY AND WEALTH

people engaged in the manufacture of lumber. What portion of the income from this industry does the South receive?

5. What proportion of the nation's industries is in the South? What percentage of southern income is derived from manufacturing? In what kinds of manufacturing does the South lead? (Give percentages of national production.) What are the evidences that manufacturing in the South is increasing?

6. Compare the amount produced by each industrial worker in the South with that of the worker in other regions of the United States; and compare the average wage received by a southern workman with that of other regions.

7. Compare the area, population, and wealth of the South with the northeastern region of the United States.

8. How may we judge the wealth of a region or measure the wealth of one region in comparison with another? Examine the indices of wealth on page 432, and compare the South with other regions, especially the Northeast, with respect to the following:
   a. Large incomes of a million or more dollars per year
   b. Wealth per capita
   c. Bank resources per capita
   d. Savings per capita
   e. Personal incomes per capita
   f. Retail sales per capita
   g. Per capita tax collection

9. Using the total number of establishments as a denominator and the number in the South as a numerator, show the South's portion of the iron and steel industries, the industries making food products, public utilities and railroad corporations, and pulp mills.

10. When the very serious financial depression made it necessary to provide emergency relief for thousands of people, how many southern states made no contribution to these funds, and how many gave an extremely small contribution? What does this indicate?

11. You have seen that the southern industrial worker receives the lowest wages, that the production per worker is lowest, that the value added by manufacture is lowest, and that other manufacturing indices place the South below other regions. Can you give and explain five or six major reasons for this?

E. Questions primarily on policy and program

1. The concentration of population in cities has generally accompanied the development and expansion of industry. In turn, the cities have presented problems of congestion, unhealthful and uncomfortable housing, concentrations of vice, crime, and delinquency. Can the South promote industrial development and avoid the problems attending urban growth?

2. Review the deficiencies summarized on pages 43 and 49 and restate in general terms the "irreducible minimum for technological development."

F. Topics for debate and forum
   1. The birth rate of the South is to blame for superabundant cheap labor.
   2. The Tennessee Valley Plan for improved farming and small industries is suggestive of what might be done throughout the South with Federal help. (In preparing this topic, consult Unit XXI.)
   3. Higher income for farmer and mill hand is needed more than anything else if their standard of living is to be raised.
   4. Exploitation by landlords and absentee owners of industry explains the low returns from southern farms and factories.

NOTES

Samplings of Indices Relating to Industry and Wealth

Number of Indices	Classification
1.	Relative standing of the states in wealth.
2.	Regional wealth—per cent of total wealth.
3.	Estimated tangible wealth per capita of the total population, by states, 1930.
4.	Per capita estimated true wealth, 1930.
5.	Per capita bank resources, 1930.
6.	Per capita postal receipts, 1930.
7.	Per capita net income of corporations, 1928.
8.	Per capita annual income, eleven-year average, 1920-1930, inclusive.
9.	Percentage distribution of income of the entire population, 1929.
10.	Per capita personal income of the entire population, 1929.
11.	Percentage distribution of income from agriculture, 1928.
12.	Percentage distribution of income from manufacture, 1928.
13.	Percentage distribution of income from mining, 1928.
14.	Percentage distribution of income from sources other than agriculture, manufacturing, and mining, 1928.
15.	Number of taxable incomes equal to, or greater than, $100,000 by states.
16.	Number of taxable incomes equal to, or greater than, $1,000,000 by states.
17.	Average federal income tax paid, 1928.
18.	Number of taxable incomes equal to, or greater than, $100,000.
19.	Number of taxable incomes equal to, or greater than, $250,000.
20.	Number of taxable incomes equal to, or greater than, $500,000.
21.	Number of taxable incomes equal to, or greater than, $1,000,000.
22.	Distribution of taxable property per capita.
23.	Amount of taxable property per capita, 1928.
24.	Ratio of all local taxes to true wealth, 1927.
25.	Percentage ratio of total state and local tax collections to the aggregate private income.
26.	Estimated state and local tax collection per capita, by state, 1930.
27.	Combined state and local government, 1930—distribution of gross receipts from license fees.
28.	Combined state and local government, 1930—ratio of license and gasoline tax to total tax collections.
29.	Combined state and local government, 1930—per capita tax collections.
30.	Relative amount of taxes and appropriations for state and local roads, 1930.
31.	Distribution of the present forest area.
32.	Distribution of the total timber stand.
33.	Distribution of the total stand, saw-timber and cordwood areas.
34.	Mineral products—differential values, by regions.
35.	Mineral products—comparative value, 1909, 1919, 1929.
36.	Comparative production of petroleum, 1930.
37.	Comparative production of natural gas, 1930.
38.	Comparative production of natural gasoline, 1930.
39.	Production of anthracite coal.
40.	Production of bituminous coal, workable.
41.	Production of bituminous coal, not workable.
42.	Comparative ore-consuming districts, 1929.
43.	Variations of concentration in the iron and steel industries, 1929.
44.	Production of building stone.
45.	Limestone products—differential values, by regions.
46.	Changing status of 12 leading states in granite sales and value of granite, 1919-1929.
47.	Comparative value of marble production, 1919-1929.
48.	Distribution of water power development—amount of horse power, 1929.
49.	Distribution of total developed water power—capacity, 1932.
50.	Per capita production of electric power, all public utility plants, 1930.
51.	Percentage distribution of the value of manufactured products, 1929.
52.	Distribution of value of products in manufacturing industries, 1929.
53.	Distribution of value added to products by manufacture, 1929.
54.	Comparative value of products in manufacturing industries, 1929.
55.	Comparative value added by manufacture in manufacturing industries, 1929.
56.	Relative increase in value of manufactured product per wage earner in manufacturing, 1914-1929.
57.	Relative increase in value of product added by manufacture, per wage earner in manufacturing, 1914-1929.
58.	Relative increase in value of manufactured product per horse power, 1914-1929.
59.	Relative increase in value of product added by manufacture, per horse power, 1914-1929.
60.	Distribution of general industrial resources—horse power.
61.	Distribution of general industrial resources—value of product.
62.	Distribution of general industrial resources—value added by manufacture.
63.	Amount and per cent of value of product added by manufacture, 1929.
64.	Amount and per cent of value of product in furniture manufacturing, 1929.
65.	Value added by manufacturing, per wage earner, in furniture manufacturing, 1929.
66.	Amount and per cent of horse power used in furniture manufacturing, 1929.
67.	Value of manufactures per horse power used in furniture manufacturing, 1929.
68.	Value of manufacture added per horse power in furniture manufacturing, 1929.
69.	Distribution of industrial establishments.
70.	Regional distribution of manufacturing establishments—textiles and their products.
71.	Regional distribution of manufacturing establishments—forest products.
72.	Regional distribution of manufacturing establishments—paper and allied products.
73.	Regional distribution of manufacturing establishments—printing, publishing, and allied products.
74.	Regional distribution of manufacturing establishments—chemical and allied products.
75.	Regional distribution of manufacturing establishments—products of petroleum and coal.
76.	Regional distribution of manufacturing establishments—leather and its manufactures.
77.	Regional distribution of manufacturing establishments—stone, clay, and glass products.
78.	Regional distribution of manufacturing establishments—railroad repair shops.
79.	Distribution of wages.
80.	Distribution of wages paid in manufacturing industries, 1929.
81.	Average annual wage per wage earner in all manufactures, 1929.
82.	Relative increase in amount of wages per wage earner in manufacturing, in three chief manufacturing regions, 1914-1929.
83.	Amount and per cent of wages paid in furniture manufacturing, 1929.
84.	Per cent of total wages per wage earner in furniture manufacturing, 1929.
85.	Non-farm population—amount, and per cent of the total, of the aggregate personal income, 1929.
86.	Non-farm population—per capita personal income, 1929.
87.	Farm population—percentage distribution of income, 1929.
88.	Farm population—per capita personal income, 1929.
89.	Cooperative sales—per cent of cash farm income, 1929.
90.	Average annual rural cash income, 1920-1930.
91.	Ratio of farm income to total income, 1930.
92.	Value of all farm property per farm, 1930.
93.	Value of land and dwellings per owned farm, 1930.
94.	Value of land and buildings per tenant farm, 1930.
95.	Value per farm of farm implements and machinery, 1930.
96.	Average agricultural production per full-time worker (year of labor) 1924-1928.
97.	Number, value per head, and total value of all cattle and calves, including cows and heifers kept for milk, 1932.

Reprinted from page 432 in *Southern Regions*.

UNIT XII

MEASURES OF INDUSTRY AND WEALTH (continued)

The South's industrial status and wealth have now been opened to view. Compared with other regions in manufacturing, the South ranks a poor third; and it ranks much lower in many specific measures of wealth. "A major deficiency is the lack of invested capital and surplus wealth to develop requisite industry. . . . The South is also a debtor region, accentuating scarcity of capital wealth through its imports from other regions of great quantities of luxuries and equipment at excess speed alongside great inequalities of income, as compared with the richer regions."

At this point it is well to look at the credit side of the account and examine the basic resources of the South and the potential industrial developments. Many factors point to shifts in the organization and location of industry. Many of the South's richest possibilities have not been appropriated for the common good.

A. Aims for the student
1. To recognize the limitations of crude indices and comparisons that emphasize quantity merely from region to region.
2. To view the real, largely hidden, potential wealth of the South that can be brought to light and wide use.
3. To analyze the factors likely to produce a shift in industrial distribution together with the industrial needs and probable developments in the southern region.
4. To confront the student with the difficulties and possibilities in such a way as to challenge him and commit him to a great undertaking—the redemption of his region from poverty.

B. Reading material for study
Southern Regions, Chapter I, pp. 81-87; Chapter VII, pp. 441-460. Review and incidental readings: pp. 35-39, 43, 47, 49, 53, 127-129, and 586.

Suggested additional reading: *Preface to Peasantry*, Chapter XIII; *Culture in the South*, Chapters XVII, XVIII, and XXIX.

C. Definitions and general guidance
See Section C in Unit XI.

D. Questions primarily on facts and mapograph interpretations

1. How does the capacity for water power in the South compare with that of other regions? Approximately, what part of this capacity is now available, and how does this compare with other regions?
2. What industry is being developed in connection with the quick-growing pine of the South? What facts point to the possible achievement of supremacy in production?
3. Explain as fully as you can the reasons underlying both clauses in the following statement from *Southern Regions:* "With the probability of considerable shift in trade routes, there is possible a new pattern for industry and wealth."
4. What are the products in world trade which are chiefly exported from the South? State especially the South's share of the exportation of cotton and naval stores. What factors indicate the likelihood of greater export development?
5. Give a general picture of the shift in industry and tell which states of the Southeast show an increase in industrial development.
6. What industrial developments based upon southern regional consumption are suggested by manufactured products now purchased outside the region?
7. What factors must be taken into consideration in determining the development of a new industry?

E. Questions primarily on policy and program

1. What are some of the proposed uses of water power, and how may agriculture and industry be changed by the transmission of power?
2. What is the major essential for the development of southern industry? What are some of the difficulties connected with offering tax exemption in order to attract capital and industry? How may capital be brought to the aid of the region?
3. What is or should be the "planning strategy for regional industry" (p. 587)?
4. In what would one expect the South to make a better showing industrially (p. 445) and what are the most obvious industrial developments open to the South?
5. What products might well be produced for both regional consumption and trade with other regions as well? What would be some first steps to take?

F. Topics for debate and forum

1. Southern industrial planning will require more than local interest and support.
2. More accurate knowledge of southern conditions and growth must be the possession of both the southerner and the non-southerner before industrial progress can be achieved in the South.
3. All cotton manufacturing should be in the South, near the base of raw materials.

NOTES

NOTES

UNIT XIII

THE SOUTHERN PEOPLE

AFTER ALL, the real wealth of a region is in its people. Whether deficiency and retardation are temporary or permanent depends to a large extent upon the basic physical strength, vitality, and the mental powers of a people. "The key picture of the southern people must be found, as in the case of the region's physical resources, in the development and use of its human resources. Like the physical resources, abounding in superquantities, these human resources await adequate institutions for their development." As with the natural wealth the chief trouble is the great gap between what might be and what is; on the one hand the region's abundance of people, their capacity for growing and doing; on the other hand the undeveloped human possibilities and tolerated waste.

To become acquainted with the southern population and to discover some of the outstanding resources and liabilities of the people is the central purpose of this unit of study. Here will be seen a picture of the numbers of people who dwell in the region as a whole and, if detailed study is pursued, in the principal subdivisions. It will be seen that the population is not so homogeneous as the expression "Southern People" would sometimes indicate, but that there are many groups representing sub-cultures or diverse patterns of life. A fuller realization of the loss and waste in human resources and of how these are related to the deficiencies and retardation of physical wealth will reward the studious observer and reader.

A. Aims for the student
1. To become familiar with the essential facts concerning southern people: total population, high birth rate, age distribution, urbanization, minority and marginal groups, and migration.
2. To see in the over-population of the South, and in the by-products of over-population: low ratio of effective producers, disproportionate educational burden, low wages, poverty, and loss through migration.
3. To recognize the essential greatness and potentiality of the southern people with their favorable lineage and biological vitality.

B. Reading material for study
Southern Regions, Chapter I, pp. 87-99; Chapter VIII, pp. 461-494. See particularly maps on pages 94, 474, 480, 14, 88, 134, 146, 484.

Suggested additional reading: *Culture in the South,* Chapters XIX, XX, XXI, and XXIII.

C. Definitions and general guidance

Ethnic: An inclusive word referring to kinship, groups, peoples, nations, tribes, or races.

Foreign-born: A resident of the United States who was born a citizen of another country.

Native-born: One who was born a citizen of the United States.

Native white: One who has a white father and a white mother.

Racial diffusion: The spreading or diffusing of the races over an area. So much diffusion and mixing of races have occurred since the dawn of humanity that no pure race can be found on the earth today.

Assimilation: This word can be understood as it is used in social science by incorporating it in a sentence thus: White America has not fully assimilated ethnic groups of different skin color, language, and culture.

Societal behavior: That behavior which nations, races, and large classes of people exhibit as contrasted with more limited social behavior. The societal behavior of man is cultural; the social behavior of ants, bees, and wasps is instinctive. The South has its societal behavior with respect to religion, politics, race, etc.

Minority group: A group of people isolated by race, creed, occupation, or location from normal participation in the advantages and control in matters of general welfare.

Wage differential: The differences in wages for similar work by reason of location, sex, or other classification of workers.

Laissez faire: A term borrowed from the French, meaning "let alone" or "let things take their course"; the viewpoint held by those who consider social, political, and economic planning as unworkable and futile.

Metropolitan district: The area surrounding a city's political boundaries, in which the work, transportation, communication, and other services of the people are dependent upon the central city. The census now provides that for cities of 100,000 population and over (in some instances 50,000) a zone of contiguous territory extending beyond the city's boundary shall be included, this territory to have at least 150 inhabitants per square mile. Therefore, the corporate area of the city plus this outer territory has been recently designated as a metropolitan district.

D. Questions primarily on facts and mapograph interpretations

1. What portion of the people in the United States live in the South? How many people are there in the region? How many of them live in cities?

THE SOUTHERN PEOPLE

How many in the highlands? What other principal groupings of the people may be made and how many are found in each?

2. How do the two southern regions compare with others as to the proportion of white people in the population? How many Negroes live in the South, and which states have the least and which the greatest proportions of colored people? Is there any significance in these facts?
3. How many Negroes live outside of the southern regions and how are they distributed by regions? Compare the growth of Negro population in the several regions of the country and state the importance of these facts.
4. How does the number of foreign-born whites compare with the number of Negroes in the United States? About what percentage of southern population is foreign-born? Has this any importance for southern culture?
5. What region has the most rapidly growing cities? How much have southern cities grown in the last ten years, and how much since 1900? How does this compare with the urban growth in the nation? How many cities of 100,000 or more people are there in the South? What southern states have the largest proportion of city dwellers?
6. For every 1,000 native white women who are 20 to 44 years of age in each of the following states write in the number of white children who are under five years of age:

   California ....   North Carolina ....
   Rhode Island ....   Alabama ....
   New York ....   South Carolina ....
   Massachusetts ....   Mississippi ....
                               Arkansas ....

   What does this table show? Why confine the ages within 20 and 44 years?
7. At what ages do people have their greatest energy and preparation for doing their most effective work? Does the South have relatively more or less of this age class than other regions? About what per cent of the people are under 19 years old in most southern states?
8. Explain how the proportions of people who are young, aged, or in the prime of life affect the productiveness, education, and pension needs of the southern region?
9. Compare the birth rate of the South with that of other regions. Can you explain how this fact is related to the proposed program for reorganizing agriculture and expanding industry?
10. What does the author mean by stating that the people of the Southeast continue to replenish other regions? Are too few people left in the South? How many have migrated since 1900? Do more men or women leave the region? What evidence is there that the South has lost excellent and alert leadership through migration? Expressed in terms of money, what has the South lost by migration in the last five years?

11. Make a statement of what the people of the South are doing. Indicate how many are engaged in agriculture; in manufacturing; in trades and transportation; and in domestic and personal service. Compare the numbers of women and children workers and the nature of their work in the South with those of other regions of the United States.
12. What factors are slowing down the migration from the South, and what attractions are likely to draw people into the region from the outside? What seems to be the probable population limits for the South in 1960? Can they be cared for under the present organization of agriculture and industry?
13. Which of the races in the South is increasing more rapidly? How does this change in ratio of numbers affect the balance of relations between the two races? Illustrate by reference to occupational changes.
14. How much less in wages do workers receive in the South for similar work to that done elsewhere? How do the facts about population help to explain this difference?
15. Name and explain five major changes in the relations of the Negro to the general life of the nation. What are some of the chief errors that have been made in thinking about races and race relations?
16. Name all the different marginal groupings of people in the South that you know and give a brief picture of the life of each.

E. Questions primarily on policy and program
1. What changes in race relations are necessary to a fair and satisfactory adjustment of race relations in the South?
2. Give several of the theories which are offered to explain the existence and increase of tenancy. Which of these do you accept, and why? How do you believe the tenancy problem should be solved?
3. If "indications are that the Southeast will have a continuing crisis in its increasingly large ratio of people" what is the immediate need, and what should be the basic solution?
4. What factors are tending to make the race problem more acute? Why is the solution of this problem likely to be delayed? What increased opportunities must be provided for Negroes if they are to be treated fairly and enabled to carry their own economic burdens?
5. Why should other regions be interested in southern education and have an obligation to contribute a part of the cost?

F. Topics for debate and forum
1. To keep the Negro in the ditch the white must stay down there with him.
2. "Behind the rallying defense of 'Let the Negro problem alone' the South has let and has forced the nation to let tenancy alone."

3. Because the lower classes always have been subservient tenants they never will make successful owners even on a small scale.
4. Population-quantity lies at the heart of most Southern economic dilemmas.
5. "The majority of these children (in marginal groups) have the capacity for strong physique and intellectual development under better environmental conditions."
6. The poor of the South have too many children. (Seven out of ten people the country over have answered "yes" to the question: "Should the distribution of information on birth control be made legal?" This proportion of affirmative answers holds for southern states as well as for other states. See press report of the Institute of Public Opinion, November 29, 1936.)
7. The South has too many people to be adequately supported on the basis of resources.

NOTES

UNIT XIV

THE EDUCATION OF THE PEOPLE

ARE SCHOOLS necessary? Why have them? Is it to be expected that they shall fix and hold the ways of the past by drilling tradition into each young generation? Or, do citizens expect schools to help each generation meet inevitable changes intelligently, and, if possible, to improve the folkways? Can education light up new paths which lead to the betterment of life, or have old paths been worn so deep that no others can be seen and appreciated? Can the South find a way out of its ruts, its numerous difficulties by the aid of education? Will schools of the South lead students to discover and develop the unused resources of the region, change wasteful practices, and distribute the benefits to all the people? Can education be merely a part of the existing pattern and simply be concerned with maintaining things as they are?

These are some of the most important questions about education, and they are not easy to answer directly. Students, and indeed the entire citizenry, will profit by getting a picture of education in the South against the background of national education in order to learn how the region ranks with others when measured by enrollment, facilities, and expenditures. It will be noted that the South's educational load is very heavy and that it has struggled heroically to achieve its present rank. Also it will be found that aid has been given to southern education from many sources outside the region. Questions will arise as to whether money and effort have been used advantageously and wisely; or whether planning is a major need along with further expansion.

A. Aims for the student
1. To get a picture of southern education with its separate organizations or agencies for sexes, races, religious denominations, geographical and political divisions, and for "practical" and liberalizing functions.
2. To determine the rank, rapidity of growth, and needed expansion by such indices as enrollment, length of term, value of property, costs of maintenance, teachers' preparation, etc.
3. To recognize the major obstacles which hinder effective education and the immediate steps necessary to counteract them.

B. **Reading material for study**

Note that the aims, reading material, and definitions for this unit apply also to the next unit which concludes the detailed study of "The Education of the People." Also questions on policy and program along with debate topics will appear in Unit XV.

Southern Regions, Chapter I, pp. 99-125; Chapter IX, pp. 502-525. Incidental readings: pp. 172, 188, 200, 230, 232, 240, 256, 312, 528, and 530, all of which are directly or indirectly related to education.

Suggested additional reading: *Culture in the South,* Chapters XI and XII; *Preface to Peasantry,* Chapters XVI, XVII, and XX.

C. **Definitions and general guidance**

Liberal education: Broad contact with all phases of human culture including languages, arts, and sciences which enable the learner to understand the origins and contents of present-day culture.

Vocational education: The focus of attention upon gaining the knowledge and skills necessary to a given business, art, or trade.

Adult education usually refers to special efforts and programs that reach grown-ups according to their particular educational needs.

Educational equalization or *equalization of educational opportunity:* The distribution of tax funds to areas according to educational need based on a consideration of the numbers to be educated regardless of the portion of funds contributed by the area. This enables areas with relative poverty and large numbers of children to offer educational opportunity equivalent to that given by the areas of greater wealth. Such distribution is justified by the fact that all areas are affected by the educational level of the mass and also because surplus populations migrate to rich areas and become citizens.

Extension work: The movement of teaching from a fixed location in a school or college to the residence or easily accessible location of the learner. Thus, teachers from a college, university, or governmental department may conduct courses of study directly in factory or home, or in the community centers of a region.

Extension service: A government or an institution, especially colleges and universities, may provide materials and expert service for the bettering of home, farm, field, and forest programs and products.

Land-grant colleges: Usually one to a state, were authorized in 1862 when federal land was granted to each state for the endowment of colleges that would emphasize agricultural and mechanical arts. From the sale of the original grants and funds added in 1890 and 1907, the states have re-

EDUCATION OF THE PEOPLE

ceived substantial funds to support the work of these colleges. One of the most recent grants came from the Bankhead-Jones Bill in 1935.

D. **Questions primarily on facts and mapograph interpretations**
   1. Previous to the depression, what were the two leading items of expense in government? What was the total cost of education for a year? About what per cent of state taxes are expended for education?
   2. Give some idea of the increase in enrollment, attendance, and accumulation of school property in comparison to the growth of national population in the last thirty years.
   3. What are the regional peculiarities which account for the lag in southern education when compared to most national indices? What facts did you learn about southern population which place unusual educational burdens upon the South?
   4. Set off against the South's portion of the national wealth and population its portion of the nation's schools and colleges, enrollment, and expenditure for the state-supported higher education.
   5. How does the school year in southern schools compare with the length of term elsewhere in the country? How does the average daily attendance during the term compare with other regions? When you consider the answers to these questions together what do they tell you about southern education?
   6. Compare teachers' salaries for the South with the national average. In the matter of costs compare Georgia with California as to the teachers' salaries, value of property per pupil, and amount spent on each pupil for a year. What educational results would you expect from these differences?
   7. Judging by the number of graduates, how rapidly have southern high schools grown in the last twenty years? How does the percentage of students who go on to high school compare with other regions? Do all children in the South have an opportunity to attend high school?
   8. Interpret the maps on pages 104, 118, 188, and 232. Then state how the maps on pages 256 and 258 may be included in the picture. What do these combined maps tell you about southern education? What is the per capita income and book circulation for southern libraries, and how does this compare with the standard? How many southern counties are without libraries? What is the population per library of 3,000 volumes in the majority of southern states?
   9. What is the length of school term in your community? What salaries are paid to teachers per year in the elementary and high schools? Where were the teachers of your community prepared for their teaching, and how long did they attend college after completing high school? How would you describe the school building or buildings in your community? Are they large enough or are they crowded? Are they beautiful inside and outside;

and do the students take pride in them? Is there plenty of playground space, well suited by grading or arrangement for the games that are played? What are the principal games, and what per cent of the students play frequently? Is there a library in your school? How many books does it have? Does it add new ones continuously or rarely? Do most of the students borrow from it or do most of them read little except their textbooks? Does your school have laboratories and special rooms? Describe these and tell whether they are well supplied or not.

10. If there is a Negro school in your community answer the same questions concerning it. Do the Negroes get about the same chance for an education as the whites? Or do they get a decidedly poorer chance?

11. Now go over the questions again and answer as many of them as you can with reference to the schools in your county. Judging from your study of the schools in the southern regions do you think those in your community and county are about average, or better than those of the region as a whole?

12. Is there a library building in your community from which all the people can borrow books? How many books are in it and what funds are used to keep it up? If there is no library building, can you get books from any library in the county or from a traveling library? Do any of the stores in your community rent books for a small sum? If you do not think your community or county is well served with books, state what you think is needed and how the community could take the first steps to make it better.

13. Summarize your picture of southern colleges, universities, and professional schools by telling:
    a. How many there are.
    b. How many are publicly supported.
    c. How much support comes from student fees.
    d. How many are for women.
    e. How many are for Negroes.
    f. How many are land-grant colleges.
    g. How teaching load and salaries compare with those of other regions.
    h. What per cent of faculties hold the Ph.D. degree.
    i. How many are among first rank in the nation.
    j. Nature of work stressed in women's colleges.
    k. Chief effects of denominational and religious influence on higher education.
    l. Principal effects of segregation of the races and of the sexes.

NOTES

NOTES

NOTES

Average Length of School Term in Days, 1927-1928

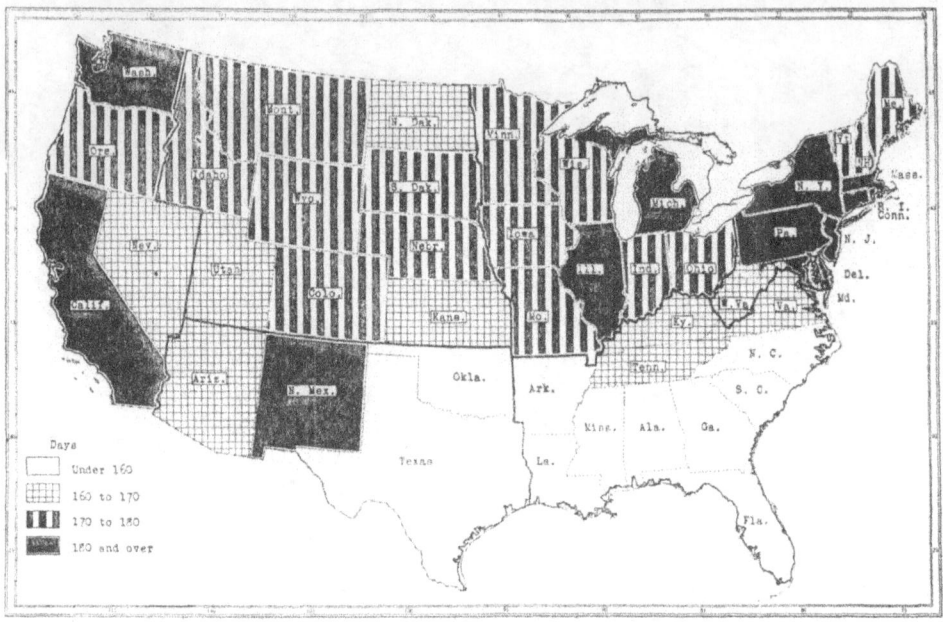

Rated according to a scale of national uniformities, Mississippi would have to expend 99.4 per cent of its tax moneys in order to reach the national average in educational standards.

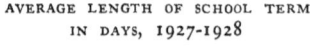

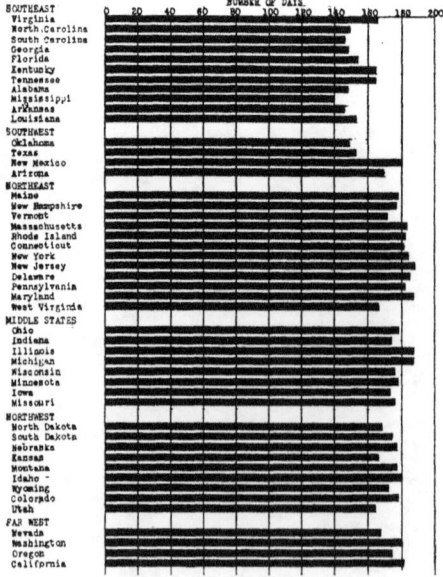

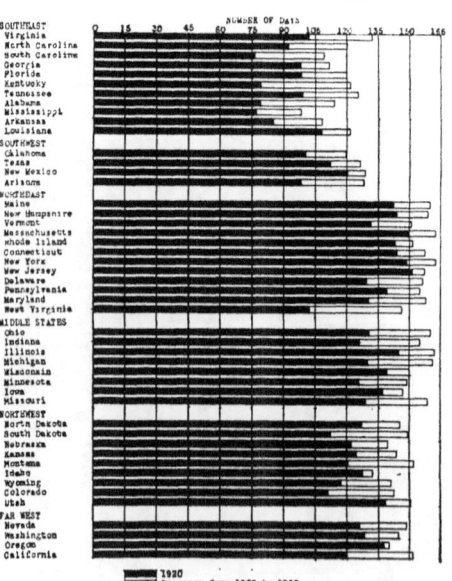

Reprinted from page 102 in *Southern Regions*.

UNIT XV

THE EDUCATION OF THE PEOPLE (continued)

THE PLACE of education in the nation and the tremendous physical and economic effort it represents should now be fairly clear. The South educationally has been compared with other regions and with the nation as a whole. For the South, the rapid growth and expansion of educational facilities and opportunities have been examined. Extra educational burdens apparently must be borne together with wastes and shortcomings. Students who have made a brief study of their own counties have possibly made an estimate of the educational position the county occupies. As a result of the study up to this point, the student should have a picture of southern education with other regions and the nation as a background, and with his own community at one side, yet in the foreground, to aid in perspective.

It is possible now to put in details and bring out special points of emphasis to complete a picture of southern education. What provision has the South made for educating its people for business and economic leadership? What are the special problems of Negro education, and what have been educational achievements of this race? Are teachers generally receiving preparation that will help them lead the South into greater realization of its possibilities, or are their eyes focused on the past? Do women receive a liberal education or a narrow training?

These and many other things the real student will wish to know. Finally, he will want to know the chief obstacles to educational development in the South and arrive at some suggestions for overcoming them.

(As noted in section B of Unit XIV, the aims, reading material, and definitions for that study apply also for this fifteenth unit.)

D. Questions primarily on facts and mapograph interpretations

1. What facts make the problem of Negro education peculiarly difficult? How does the status of Negro education affect the educational rank of the southern region in general? Describe the progress of Negro education by pointing out the value of property and amount of endowment which has been raised. What are the numbers of Negro students and teachers, and how effectively has illiteracy been reduced among Negroes? What are the principal effects of Negro education on each of the races in the South?

2. With the exception of a few institutions such as Wesleyan College of Macon, Georgia, why was the South slow to make provision for the education of women, especially for higher education? Are there evidences that the region still approves of less or different education for its women? How many women's colleges are found in the South and how does the percentage of women's colleges in the South compare with other regions? What is the significance of the fact that most women's colleges are under private or denominational control? Compare the material that is taught or emphasized in southern women's colleges with that offered by such colleges in other regions.

3. In what southern states are the state agricultural colleges separated from the universities? What points of emphasis have grown out of this separation, and what false conceptions have developed concerning these two agents of public education? Point out the probable gain or loss to the states by having such a separation.

4. Recall the rank of the South in industry and then state its approximate rank in schools of commerce and business. What are the evidences that the South is or is not well prepared to furnish adequately trained leaders and assistants for a fairly rapid industrial expansion?

5. From what sources outside the region has the South received funds and stimulation for its educational development? What Funds have contributed especially to Negro education? Give some idea of the amounts which have been contributed by the General Education Board and Rockefeller Foundation to southern education. What educational efforts in the South have been made possible largely through grants by the federal government?

6. How does the emphasis upon extension work in the South compare with other regions? State whether you think this emphasis is justified and give your reasons. What other direct or original educational projects have been developed in the South? What is their probable significance?

7. Have normal schools in the South paid particular attention to the development of leaders and teachers who can deal effectively and constructively with southern problems? What has been stressed most by normal schools in their educational program?

8. What have been the most noticeable effects of the depression upon southern education? Which of these appear to you most serious and why do you regard them as such?

9. What are the chief obstacles, other than limited financial resources, to a full realization of educational development and educational effectiveness in the Southern regions? How can you assist in overcoming these obstacles? What are some of the most reasonable remedies?

10. What are the principal handicaps of teachers and educational administrators

in the South? What notable achievements have they made in spite of those handicaps?

E. Questions primarily on policy and program
1. What procedures are proving effective in changing and reorganizing the culture of the southern regions more rapidly than schools and colleges seem able to do? What agencies are demonstrating the power of setting up examples or alternate patterns of living as a means of inducing constructive change?
2. What factors are likely to produce changes in the number and relations of small colleges in the South? What seems to you an ideal function and arrangement of small colleges in a regional organization of education?
3. What would be the value of having a private university of the first rank in the South and in what sense is this an immediate major goal for regional education?
4. Does the picture derived from your summary in question 13 of Unit XIV suggest any need for planning and reorganizing the agencies of higher education in the South? What are some of the rather obvious improvements which you think should be made?
5. Set forth the educational goals which the South should undertake to reach during the next five years.
6. Explain the regional and national importance of educational equalization.

F. Topics for debate and forum
1. "Southern culture is immature rather than decadent."
2. Education of children is more than a local concern, it is the responsibility of state and nation.
3. The four L's: literacy, libraries, liquor, and lynching. (Maps on pp. 104, 118, 568, and 146.)
4. Without an adequate educational base the structure of religion, science, and government cannot stand.
5. "In the political culture of the South inhere the limitations of educational support."
6. "The Southeast may well consider . . . one or more well supported municipal universities."
7. "The region need not lag on the one hand, nor, on the other, follow blindly the paths of a hectic, urban, technological, transitional period of civilization."
8. The South should hold out for continuation of the classical liberal education.
9. The South should continue its emphasis upon colleges for women.

NOTES

NOTES

UNIT XVI

POLITICAL GENIUS AND GOVERNMENT FINANCE

THIS PART of the study presents a comparative picture of colorful southeastern folkways in the administration of government, both state and national. In a sense the picture is one of contrasts as well as of comparisons. Questions such as these may come to mind: Has the South maintained its former peerless leadership in national affairs? Is the South in its congressional power today and tomorrow going to continue to compare favorably with other portions of the country? What must be done to insure fine leadership? Will a better type of political guidance develop with a changing political scene? Is the single party system something that should be encouraged? Do we want real competition in politics as well as in business or do we want monopoly? Is it a choice between challenge and invigoration on the one hand and unquestioning acceptance and stagnation on the other hand? Can the South possibly stir the currents of new life without wise leadership, without the willingness to dig deep into its own resources of mind and men, of materials and money, and then invest confidently in itself even as other peoples have done through hard work and taxes?

Leadership and new attitudes will be both cause and effect of improved, perhaps reformed, folkways. Problems of status, of privilege, of opportunity, of fair dealing enter here. They are what has been termed by Dr. Odum and others, the problems of "unequal places." Are there unequal places which must be more nearly levelled off in the interests of a New South?

Can the rights of childhood, the needs of the impoverished tenant, or the plight of the Negro be detached from the political and financial aspects of the total picture? Constitutional privileges and protections may be written without regard to age, status, race, or creed but are they not too often nullified by localism? Is there occasionally the evidence of gross inequality or imbalance between what *may* be and what *must* be? May the child be entitled to an adequate education at public expense; must he be satisfied with five or six months of school in the year? May every really qualified person have the right to exercise his citizenship through the ballot? Must he be careful how he asserts this right? Must every property holder pay taxes whether his child gets a fair share of educational expenditure or not; whether he himself has the right to vote?

While the darker phases of the political, educational, and racial situations are rather well and widely known, the brighter side is not always held to view. The South has been digging some new channels of thought and action, has really been at work in righting wrongs, and has been enjoying a growing respect for law and order. Educational inequality has been attacked with vigor and results; tenancy is under the searching study of the South's own local and congressional leaders; and the race problem is in many places less grievous than ever before because of new knowledge and interracial coöperation. Tolerance and justice appear to be on the way toward higher honor.

Concretely there are other promising signs. The Southeast makes a favorable showing in the amount of taxes raised in proportion to income. In view of the relatively lower income rates, the comparatively high tax rate may not indicate a wholly fortunate situation. Certain it is that the South has farther to go and more to carry. The degree of efficiency of state and local governments as compared with other sections also brings up the question as to whether the tax dollar in the South goes as far as in other sections. What about the many counties doubtless needed in a horse-and-buggy age? Does the continued dominance of one party make for governmental economy or for costly inefficiency? How can such problems, if problems they are, be solved?

Coöperative democracy? Is the enlightened southern mind—northern mind, western mind, *American mind*—likely to grant permanence to political dictation that would imperil democratic foundations? Has the South had more than its share of political demagogues and rabble-rousers? If so, why? Certainly this is true: The South has men and women of fine discrimination, of splendid tolerance and high ability; it has human and natural resources that can be transmuted into priceless wealth; and its people can with vision and coöperative effort open up avenues of wise expenditure so that democracy will become a reality throughout the region and the republic.

A. Aims for the student
1. To account for the series of contrasts present in the South with respect to the absence of national leadership and the presence of congressional leadership.
2. To glimpse some of the reasons why the South has so much violence and yet has earned for the region the title, "Bible Belt."
3. To evaluate the single party system and the apparent waste and inefficiency in local and state systems of government.

4. To account for the high tax rate and high rate of tax collection contrasted with the small expenditures for education.
5. To explain the small expenditures for education and the liberal outlays for roads and highways.

B. Reading material for study
Southern Regions, Chapter I, pp. 125-135; Chapter IX, pp. 525-527.

Suggested additional reading: *Culture in the South*, Chapters VII and XXX.

C. Definitions and general guidance
National leadership is here taken to refer to the executive branch of the federal government rather than to the congressional or legislative branch. For example, the South has not had a president for the last sixty years, nor have there been in that period presidential candidates from any party who were residing in the South at the time their candidacy was announced.

Political demagogue: One who seeks to control or does control a political unit without regard to regular parliamentary procedure; also one who is intolerant of ideas and points of view other than his own, and who may resort to popular prejudices to gain his political goal.

Index number: A device for reducing data to a rating scale for the sake of making definite comparisons. For example, in measuring economic production year after year, some one year is generally taken as a base, such as, $1926 = 100$. Annual fluctuations in production can thus be measured in terms of the 1926 level as being the "normal" year.

Tax, taxation: The purpose of taxation is to meet the public needs of government. Here is one of the most difficult and intricate phases of modern economics and politics; ideally the burden of taxation should be based upon "ability to pay"; actually taxes usually filter down, are passed on, and are hidden in selling prices and rents, with the result that everyone pays taxes whether he is aware of it or not. Someone has suggested that today tax feathers are plucked from our American Eagle where the plucking is likely to produce the least squawk.

Poll tax: Usually applies to every male person at age twenty-one and thereafter, indicating his right to vote.

Sales tax: Usually less than 5 per cent and payable by the purchaser of goods at retail; a form of taxation generally disapproved because of its heavy burden upon the poor, and looked upon as a temporary device to obtain revenue that "ought" to be raised otherwise by the government.

Income tax: A percentage of a person's money income may be demanded by state and national government, sometimes graduated according to ability to pay.

Excise tax: Revenue from commodities and activities such as tobacco, liquor, sports, etc.; *internal revenue taxes* is another term.

Severance tax: This has to do with extraction of natural products, as in forestry, mining, etc.

D. Questions primarily on facts and mapograph interpretations

1. Why do so many lawyers go into politics?
2. Think of the South in comparison with other sections of the country as to national leadership. Is the falling off in leadership due to the Civil War or to other situations and conditions? Explain.
3. Describe the rôle of the South with respect to leadership in Congress. Can it be termed statesmanship or something else?
4. Account for the relative prominence of southern congressional leaders as contrasted with the almost total absence of presidential aspirants from the South since the Civil War.
5. Compare the Southeast with other sections of the United States with regard to tax increases per capita and tax collections per capita.
6. Compare governmental expenditures in the Southeast with similar expenditures in other sections as to (a) general government; (b) protection to persons and property; (c) development and conservation of natural resources; (d) conservation of health and sanitation; (e) highways; (f) charities and hospitals; (g) education; (h) recreation; (i) public service.
7. Compare income tax of the Southeast with other sections of the United States. What are the differences and why?
8. Compare bonded indebtedness in the Southeast with other regions. What are the differences and why?
9. Compare the status of the Southeast with other areas with respect to woman suffrage in 1919; prohibition in 1917; Fordney-McCumber Tariff (Republican high tariff) in 1921; Hawley-Smoot Tariff (Republican, still higher tariff amid protest of economic experts) in 1930; and Underwood Tariff (Democratic, lower tariff) in 1913.
10. List recent political demagogues of the South. How many were lawyers? Ministers? Business men? Farmers?
11. To what extent do the South's registered voters fall behind other areas in terms of total population to the number of registered voters?
12. To what extent does the refusal to allow the Negro to register account for the situation implied in question 11?
13. Compare the South with other sections as to the number of lynchings (a) white; (b) colored. Is lynching necessary to serve the ends of justice? Why?

E. Questions primarily on policy and program

1. What are some of the most promising ways of creating taxable wealth in the southern regions?
2. How are politics and economics dependent upon each other in any plan for the wealth progress of the South?
3. Is political demagoguery something that people want or something that they tolerate? What is the best way to change conditions that encourage demagoguery?
4. Which should be more important in the next few years, school-mindedness or road-mindedness? Why? (Contrast expenditures for highways and education, especially in Arkansas, Tennessee, and South Carolina, with expenditures for highways and education in Delaware, Minnesota, and Utah. How do you account for the relatively greater expenditure for education in Delaware, in Minnesota, and in Utah, and a relatively greater expenditure for highways in Arkansas, Tennessee, and South Carolina?)
5. Is a regional policy of remaining "solid" politically likely to be in the direction of progress? Why?

F. Topics for debate and forum

1. The South may well heed the words of an eminent Irish leader in speaking of the South of Ireland: "We are too poor not to provide for the education of the people."
2. "Taxes? My state needs highways, not higher education."
3. The South lags behind in national affairs because it lacks good leaders.
4. The South needs two political parties, regardless of national politics.
5. Illiteracy begets demagoguery.
6. White supremacy demands that whites, though ignorant, shall vote rather than allow Negroes, though intelligent, to become voting citizens.
7. "Taxpayer, Meet Your County" (*Survey Graphic*, August, 1936; also *Readers Digest*, September, 1936). Fewer counties plus more county managers will mean economy and efficiency.

NOTES

Composition of Southeastern States' Legislative Representatives

Adapted from a special inquiry made by W. C. Jackson for the Southern Regional Study

DISTRIBUTION	Virginia	North Carolina	South Carolina	Georgia	Florida	Kentucky	Tennessee	Alabama	Mississippi	Arkansas	Louisiana
Number of Members	100	120	124	205	95	100	100	106	140	100	100
Democrats	90	112	124	193	94	74	83	80		100	100
Republicans	4	8		11	1	26	17	2			
Independents	1			1				2			
Women	1	1		2					3	1	
Average Age		42.27				51.3	45	49.1	43.4	45.13	
Youngest		24				26	24	25	23	22	
Oldest		76				82	74	82	82	71	
Under 30 Years		7				7	17	6	34	12	
Born in State	88	111	115	190	48	97	87	80	123	76	86
Born in:											
Virginia		1	1	3	4				1		
North Carolina	2		6	3	2		1				
South Carolina		2		3	2				2		
Georgia	1	1	1		18		2	4		1	
Florida				2					1		
Kentucky					2		1		2		
Tennessee		1		1	1			1	2	3	3
Alabama			1	2	5					1	1
Mississippi					1		5	2		6	4
Arkansas							2		1		1
Louisiana					1				2		
Born Out of South		2		1	7	3	2		3	12	5
Born Abroad	1	1			4			1		1	2
Rural Residence	58	70	74	119	49		50	58	101	55	50
Urban under 40,000	25	38	40	70	38		26	32	37	42	28
Urban over 40,000	17	12	10	16	8		21	14	2	3	22
Military Service	22	23	16	27	24	8		13	14		
Secret Orders		65				41		70	130		
College Training	66	76	65	103	53	17		47			
Previous Service:											
in House	62	59	49	50	31	36		36	29		
in Senate		10	2	7		1			2		
in Both	1	8	2	18	3	3			4		
in Congress		1									
as Lieutenant Governor		1									
as Speaker		1									
Previous Office Holder	33	25	42		48	36		38			
Religion:											
Methodist	28	29		69	37	17	24	40	39	36	
Baptist	25	35		80	19	26	25	21	55	21	
Episcopalian	18	10		2	7		1	1	6	3	
Presbyterian	13	21		13	5	10	14	7	25	10	
Christian	5			3	3	15	14		1	5	
Catholic	1				1	5		3	1	2	2
Church of Brethren	1										
Methodist Protestant		2									
Primitive Baptist		3		5	2	1	2	1	1		
Disciple		1									
Lutheran		3		2			1			1	
Friend		1									
Church of God		1									
Jew		1			3	1	2			1	
Disciple of Christ				1		1				1	
Congregational						1	1	1			
Latter Day Saint						1					
Church of Christ						2	3	1		5	
United Brethren							3				
Evangelical						1					
Campbellite						1					
Universalist								1			
Protestant									1	5	
Holiness										1	
Unitarian										1	
Not Given	4	13				11	10	10	8		
Lawyers	47	46	34	64	42	17	28	41	42	31	31
Professions other than Law	7	8	14	17	10	17	12	8	18	16	9
Farming and Planting	18	31	43	41	17	24	35	17	36	23	20
Business	19	28	25	36	23	31	19	16	31	20	27
Labor	1		7		2	2	2	1	3	3	11
Miscellaneous	3	4		5	1	2	4	1	7	1	1

Blank spaces indicate no data. Due to the fact that data were not available on all individuals the classifications do not always add to the totals.

UNIT XVII

PUBLIC AND PRIVATE SOCIAL SERVICES

THE DEGREE of social responsibility manifested by a people is likely to be a reflection of their general culture. A progressively-minded people will be actively aware of mounting problems that need attention. Those who are yesterday-minded seldom sense the larger needs of alterations in manners and methods in order to meet changing situations. Progress is, of course, not easy to define; so much depends on one's point of view, the place, and the people concerned. To plan the wholesale slaughter of drug addicts does not conform to American ideas of progress, but it may be a sanctioned procedure for the Chinese. To put an old parent in an institution for the aged is unthinkable to most Chinese; not so with many Americans. The folkways of a people or a region cannot be understood without a study of their culture.

Neighborliness and local charity were prominent features of earlier American culture, sufficient for the time and conditions. But in the more complex living of today can they be adequate to answer the needs of multitudes? Think of the importance of prevention, protection, correction, and restoration; of fires, floods, and pestilences that threaten so many people. Adversity that all but engulfs large portions of the population must be systematically approached and attacked. Many children, mothers, and old folks, the sick in body and mind, the delinquent, the criminal, and the victims of disaster—all need society's help. In former days neighborly mutual aid was sufficient, but today it can do little more than supply the motive for more comprehensive programs.

Is the South an exception? Can the South get along without organized social work? Can the church meet the need? Is general philanthropy enough? Would the church and philanthropy even surpass their former good works by incorporating the best that science and social work have to offer? Can it be wisely said that the South is still rather personal and face-to-face in its relationships and that for this reason the "impersonal" programs of public welfare (the social work aspect of government) and social service (private organized effort) are not so much needed as in other areas?

Since all social service is so largely a community concern it must be thought of in that connection. What about segregated groups and unequal places? Can real democracy allow any human being to be "passed by on the other side"?

The South has provided pioneering leadership in social work. The first county unit plan of public welfare was established in North Carolina in 1918. Country-wide attention was attracted to what was being done for whites and blacks. Here was the first statewide system to get into operation following a plan, it should be said, copied in part from Jackson County, Missouri, a border state between North and South.

Today the federal government seems to be on the threshold of far-reaching social service in its program of social security. With the development of social services by the central government it should be possible to coördinate state and federal programs so as to achieve efficiency as never before, and to do it for all concerned, the people and their government. The plans whereby the states must contribute a part of the funds before federal appropriations are available should enable all regions to make considerable progress in professional organization of social services.

A. Aims for the student
  1. To examine the facts relating to the inferior support of public welfare and social service in the Southeast as compared with other sections.
  2. To evaluate the place of women and children in the southern picture.
  3. To account for the attitudes and practices that persist in connection with the criminal, especially the chain gang.

B. Reading material for study
  Southern Regions, Chapter I, pp. 135-141; Chapter V, pp. 371-373.

  Suggested additional reading: *Culture in the South*, Chapter XXXI.

C. Definitions and general guidance
  Age of consent: The age at which one is considered competent to give (legal) consent to marriage or to unlawful sex behavior usually involving an adult and a child, especially a young girl. A child is not considered competent to give consent today until the age of sixteen or eighteen. Formerly at common law the age was as low as ten years, but now it has been raised by statute in most states.

  Delinquency: A newer synonym for criminality especially as it pertains to youth. Rather than to describe children by the harsh word "criminal," the offending, wayward young are referred to as juvenile delinquents.

Mothers' Aid: Statutory provision for financial assistance by the state to enable mothers of children whose fathers have died or deserted to keep the home intact. The emphasis is upon the welfare of the child. Earlier terms were such as "mothers' pension," "widows' pension," "mothers' assistance," and "mothers' compensation."

Ideology: The science of patterning of ideas. For example, the ideology of the politician may be quite in contrast to that of the social scientist.

Vocational rehabilitation broadly defined deals with different types of handicapped persons; aims at remunerative placement or re-establishment in the economic world; implies advice and training for occupations. "Re-education" has a similar meaning. The problem of the square-peg-in-the-round-hole, of directing the criminal's destructive skills into constructive activity, of helping those who may not be able otherwise to keep up with their fellows.

Parole is the plan whereby a person is released from a correctional institution before his regular sentence has expired. He remains theoretically a prisoner, subject to recommitment if he violates the parole agreement. The philosophy underlying the practice of parole assumes that, if properly applied, parole may do more toward rehabilitating the offender than would be accomplished if the offender served the entire term in prison.

Pardon is the procedure whereby the person is relieved of further responsibility for the offense for which he was committed. He is given his freedom. Citizenship's rights may or may not be restored with the pardon. The pardoning power usually rests with the governor or a pardon board.

Public welfare, public social service is that form of social work undertaken and supported by some unit of government—city, county, state, or federal. Public social service, therefore, is social service supported through taxation.

Private social service, on the other hand, is the type of social work that is supported by private funds, such as contributions of individuals for the support of an agency through a community fund.

The National Conference of Social Work is an organization for the promotion of social service as a profession. It was organized in 1873 as the National Conference of Charities and Corrections. The name was later changed to the National Conference of Social Work.

D. **Questions primarily on facts and mapograph interpretations**
   1. What is the condition of probation and parole work in the Southeast? What makes the crime problem in the South more burdensome than in the North?
   2. What is the chain gang? Why did it develop in the Southeast and what

may be said of the system as a method of treatment of crime? What relation, if any, does the system have to slavery? to climate?
3. Compare institutional expenditures for the insane and feeble-minded in the Southeast with other sections.
4. Compare expenditures for social service in the Southeast with other areas. How likely is it that the need is less, therefore the expense is less?
5. Account for the slowness of the Southeast in providing for social services. What part did or does religion play? politics?
6. Account for the unfavorable comparison of the Southeast with other areas with respect to contributions to social services.
7. To what extent do inadequate social services, illiteracy, and areas of low per capita incomes run hand in hand? Illustrate.

E. Questions primarily on policy and program
1. Will it be necessary for states, perhaps the federal government, in the future to provide a type of "equalization fund" to take care of the relief needs of certain poorer areas that may be unable to meet the expenses of local relief requirements?
2. In what ways can politics be a hindrance to public welfare progress? Are there any indications that science, rather than politics, is becoming influential in the government's social work programs?
3. Would two or more political parties of comparatively equal strength tend to promote a more comprehensive system of social services?

F. Topics for debate and forum
1. It is the responsibility of government to provide jobs so that all able-bodied persons will support themselves and their dependents.
2. Concentration camps in charge of army officers should be established for the transient, the shiftless, and the generally worthless. Rigid work and discipline in such camps should be the order of the day.
3. The Democratic party has been responsible for the relative slowness in providing adequate social services in the Southeast.
4. Negroes should be as amply provided for in matters of relief as whites.
5. Negro social workers should receive as high salaries for the same degree of professional social work training as white social workers.
6. The orphanage, an institution so characteristic of the South, is the best way to care for parentless children.

NOTES

HOMICIDES, 1918-1927

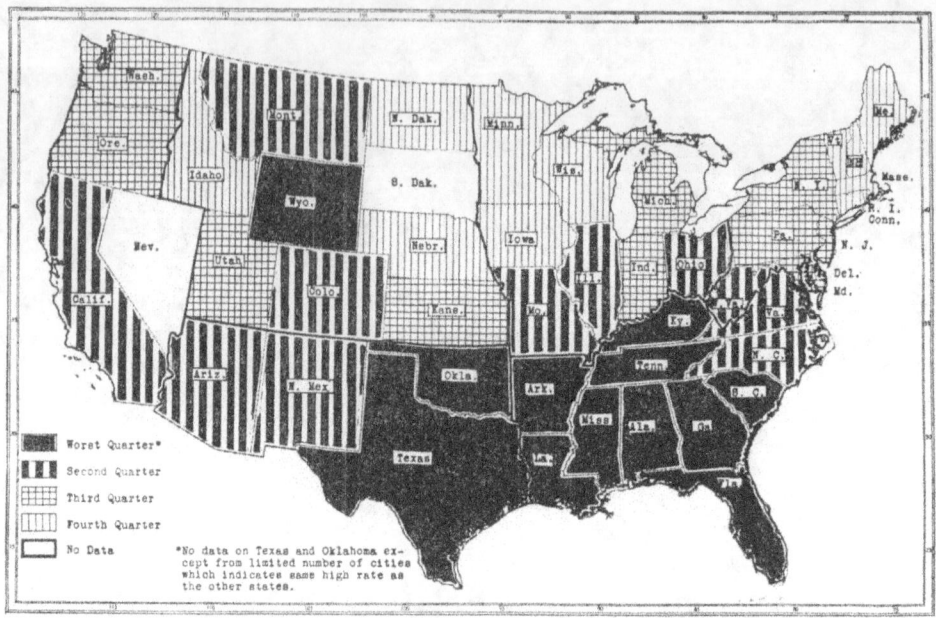

The Southeast reflects the Protestant preponderance, being characterized somewhat as early American in its religion and stocks of people, other than Negroes. The folkways of the frontier, of "honor," of white supremacy, however, have not hitherto run contrary to the religious motivation of the region.

LYNCHINGS, 1889-1932

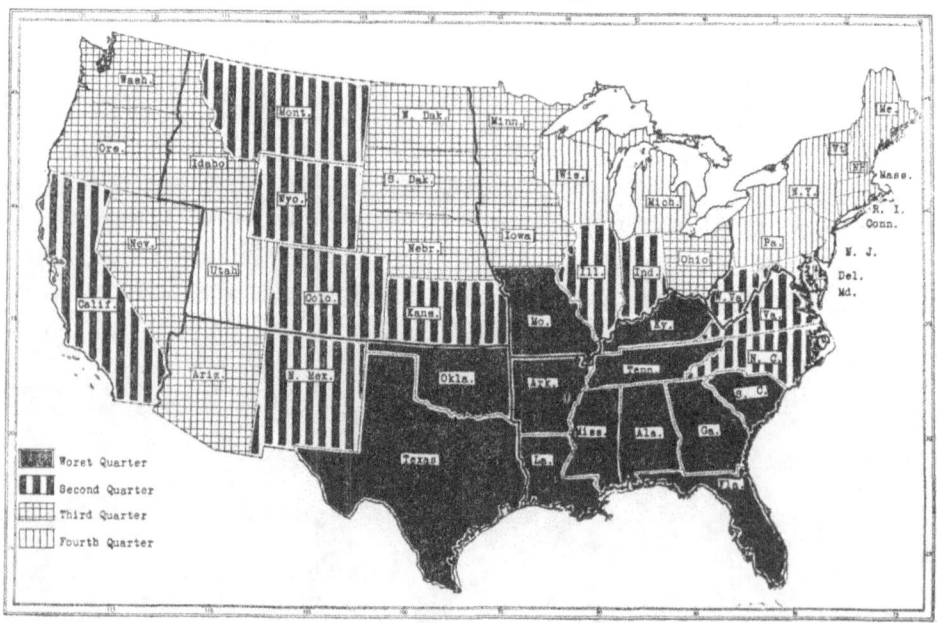

Reprinted from page 146 in *Southern Regions*.

UNIT XVIII
RELIGION AND CULTURE

IN RELIGION no solid South exists today. The two regions and some of the smaller areas differ among themselves and from each other. The Southeast, stronghold of Protestantism, ranks at the top of the six regions in enrolled church membership, while the Southwest stands in fourth position with a considerable number of Roman Catholics. The South as a whole has a larger number of small churches, buildings and memberships, than any other area of the country. This great number of churches to be supported by few financially poor members means very often a costly drain for the upkeep of church property and support of ministers. An excessive supply of churches invites problems of quality in preaching and leading, in music, and in local activities. Coöperative community effort may be difficult where many church steeples point surely the "right" way. Do these words from *An American Epoch* correctly sketch a part of the picture:

> The first third of the twentieth century showed the chief pattern of the South to be still preëminently religious, and primarily a worldly religion of self-righteousness, although the South was undoubtedly unconscious of it. "Southern" Christianity was the index of all Christianity. Like southern Democracy, it was being measured by the measuring rods of "our" Christianity, that is, agreeing with "our" ideas, concepts, and practices. In fact, it was often assumed that a cosmopolitan or world Christianity or world brotherhood, ordinarily considered basic in the principles of Christianity, were opposed to many of the ideals of "southern" Christianity. This was in part heritage of a conflict between North and South and between white and Negro, which made the complete brotherhood of man, except in foreign fields, untenable. The southern Christianity was generous in its treatment of foreigners abroad, but hard on foreigners in America. And upon all questions, political, financial, educational, scientific, and technical, the judgment of religion and the scriptures was likely to be invoked.

If this was true of the first three decades of the century, will it continue to be so for the fourth and fifth?

How can extremes of religious expression be explained in terms of culture? How much justification is there for such journalistic taunts as that about the "Bible Belt," or for verses that laugh at August "meetin's"?

Other questions there are: Why not more churches with an emphasis on the vitalities of the social gospel; why so much literalism and so little liberalism; why so much dogmatism and so little open-minded search for truth? Let it be made clear that these questions issue not only from the South itself, from other parts of America, but also from abroad. They are questions that should not be warmly dismissed; rather they should be given thoughtful consideration. In the face of all this questioning there is evidence that in many southern communities both pulpit and pew are heading toward greater tolerance of other faiths, more brotherhood in practice, and more reasoned religious beliefs.

A. Aims for the student
1. To note the regional and subregional differences and variations in religious expression the country over.
2. To account for the divergencies between religious preachment and social practice.
3. To examine the possibilities of bringing about more community and less sectarian emphasis in religion, so that scattered strength and resources may be brought into more power and usefulness for the people today.

B. Reading material for study
Southern Regions, Chapter I, pp. 141-149; Chapter IX, pp. 501-502; 525-527.

Suggested additional reading: *Culture in the South*, Chapter XIII; *Liberalism in the South*, Chapters II, XI, and XVI; *Time, Matter and Values*, by R. A. Millikan; *An American Epoch*, Chapter XII, by Howard W. Odum.

C. Definitions and general guidance
Religion (and science): Religion is a part of the general culture of a people; expresses itself in many ways wherever man is found in ethnic groups. It involves belief in unseen, superhuman power to which or to whom man feels himself in some degree accountable. Enlightened present-day Christianity and other enlightened religions emphasize belief and practice, faith and works, conduct here as well as reward hereafter. Religion ventures faith in God; science puts its faith in law. Both religion and science seek after truth; they recognize an ordered, lawful universe in which change and growth are the vital processes.

Time-lag relates to people and conditions that start late or move slowly in relation to others of their kind. It may be said that among human-kind the American Negro in three hundred years of white culture has overcome remarkably the time-lag caused by thousands of years of side-tracking in Africa. The time-lag in southern education as compared with other regions is slowly being reduced in a few states. Yet "the Southeast is as the whole nation was in the earlier decades to the extent that agricultural ways of life predominate."

D. Questions primarily on facts and mapograph interpretations
1. Criticize this logic: There are very few Roman Catholics in the South; there is very much violence in the South; therefore, if there were more Roman Catholics there would be less violence. (See p. 144.)
2. Criticize this logic: The South is predominantly Methodist and Baptist (p. 140); the South is also predominant in lynchings and homicides (p. 146); therefore, Protestants do not believe in the Sixth Commandment.
3. Is there any relation between illiteracy and denominationalism, great numbers of churches, and much church attendance (pp. 104, 140, and 144)?
4. On the top half of page 526 what do you find that is regionally significant about the average number of members per church and the per cent of churches whose pastors serve from one to six churches?
5. In what particulars is religion in the South an expensive dichotomy? Think of denominations, racial factors, and their connection with education.
6. What might be the reason that Methodist and Baptist churches have such a following in the South? Why are there relatively few independent churches of the Quaker and Congregational type that are noted for their conservative worship patterns and ceremonies?
7. Explain why the great majority of Negroes in the South are either Baptists or Methodists.
8. Can the map on the lower half of page 568 be explained in terms of religion? or is it otherwise explainable?
9. Is the South suffering from any time-lag in religion? Explain.

E. Questions primarily on policy and program
1. Is there more justification for numerous small churches in areas of scattered population than in compact communities? Why? Why not run busses for a consolidated church in rural areas as well as for school?
2. In ———ville the population is 650, of whom 350 range from babyhood to youth, 200 from 20 to 45 years, and 100 from 45 to old age. The five churches are hard to heat, harder to fill, without equipment that appeals to young people, most of the pews are empty on Sunday, the edifices are closed throughout the week except for occasional meetings and for regular prayer meeting. All five ministers preach from the Bible and the members accept the Christian faith. What should be done in this situation?
3. How can the richness and beauty of the New Testament be made more real in southern life? Could the life and teachings of Jesus be somehow made

a part of the public school program? Give some arguments for and against.
4. What would be a good plan in line with the third aim of this unit? Think of pastor, building, equipment, location, social activities, etc., in your own local situation.

F. **Topics for debate and forum**
 1. Religion and science have little in common.
 2. The Bible, the hymnbook, and the almanac are sufficient. (See second paragraph of Unit IV.)
 3. Tax supported welfare programs have been retarded by the "charities" of the churches.

NOTES

NOTES

Percentage of Methodists and Baptists in Total Church Membership, 1926

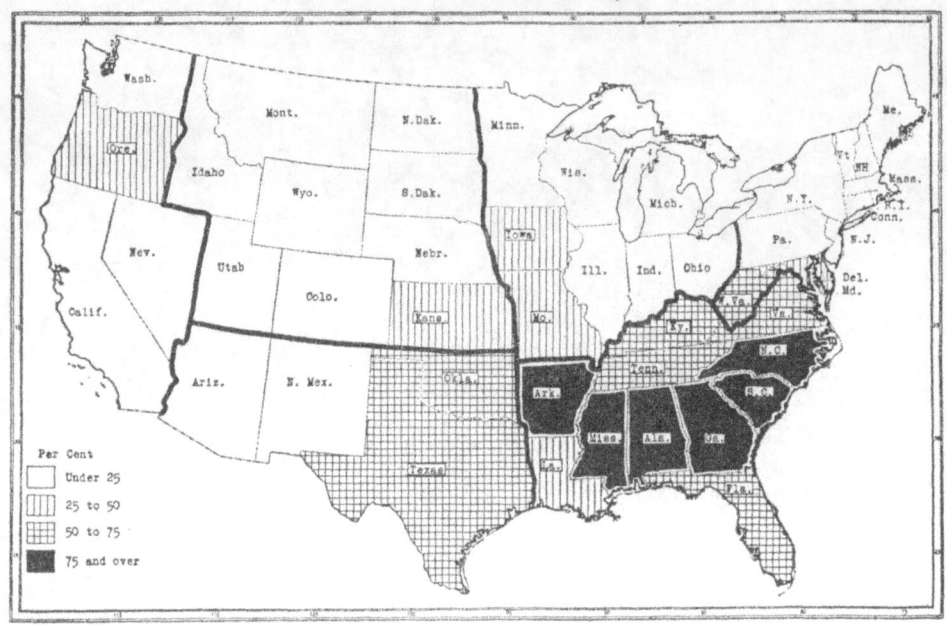

Distribution of Jews, Adult Catholics, and Adult Members of Church of Jesus Christ of Latter-Day Saints, by States and Regions, 1926*

STATE	Jews	Adult Catholics	Adult Members Church of Jesus Christ of Latter-Day Saints	STATE	Jews	Adult Catholics	Adult Members Church of Jesus Christ of Latter-Day Saints
Southeast........	125,850	693,341	17,869	*Middle States*...	773,749	3,876,261	6,868
Virginia...........	22,414	27,298	1,456	Ohio.............	166,154	678,851	550
North Carolina....	3,724	4,851	1,631	Indiana...........	23,622	224,789	828
South Carolina....	3,956	6,221	2,581	Illinois...........	339,730	970,853	1,822
Georgia...........	18,366	13,178	2,662	Michigan.........	83,161	591,672	765
Florida...........	11,975	28,838	2,037	Wisconsin........	31,839	453,888	478
Kentucky.........	15,548	126,047	1,656	Minnesota.......	39,925	333,133	492
Tennessee.........	18,993	18,566	1,857	Iowa.............	12,714	207,277	438
Alabama..........	9,218	27,213	1,561	Missouri..........	76,604	415,798	1,495
Mississippi........	2,871	22,557	1,256				
Arkansas..........	4,940	17,027	183	*Northwest*......	42,311	544,068	343,428
Louisiana.........	13,845	401,545	989	North Dakota....	1,626	65,278	100
				South Dakota....	380	67,592	539
Southwest.......	44,487	603,539	15,926	Nebraska........	12,271	109,170	523
Oklahoma.........	4,098	33,313	422	Kansas...........	4,973	121,358	......
Texas.............	39,089	390,952	2,112	Montana.........	671	49,577	1,763
New Mexico......	367	115,005	1,084	Idaho............	316	16,268	64,042
Arizona...........	933	64,269	12,308	Wyoming.........	834	13,352	8,511
				Colorado.........	18,950	90,498	4,273
Northeast.......	2,930,907	6,826,261	3,849	Utah.............	2,290	10,975	263,677
Maine............	7,582	118,197	......				
New Hampshire...	2,129	106,651	......	*Far West*.......	147,938	685,715	28,205
Vermont..........	1,433	64,841	......	Nevada...........	164	6,066	3,402
Massachusetts....	213,085	1,206,999	407	Washington......	13,050	88,415	4,100
Rhode Island.....	24,034	235,511	......	Oregon..........	12,000	40,997	5,159
Connecticut......	90,165	409,513	122	California........	122,724	550,237	15,544
New York........	1,899,597	2,289,093	1,106				
New Jersey.......	219,455	749,422	......	United States....	4,081,242†	13,278,900†	417,810†
Delaware.........	5,000	27,422	......				
Pennsylvania.....	393,517	1,399,153	723				
Maryland.........	69,974	170,284	479				
West Virginia.....	4,936	49,175	1,012				

*Census of Religious Bodies, 1926. These three faiths are classified as non-protestant, all others being protestant according to the census definition. Jewish congregations did not report members according to age distribution.
†District of Columbia included.

Reprinted from page 140 in *Southern Regions*.

UNIT XIX

ASPECTS OF GENERAL CULTURE

WITH A FEW exceptions the main aspects of culture have already been emphasized and studied. Earlier units have been given to the study of cultural equipment and problems; later ones to special examination of agriculture, industry, education, government, social service, and religion. These main heads nearly complete a framework of culture but there is one foundation institution that as yet has not been directly viewed—the Family. Nor can this most essential institution be studied here with any completeness but only with regard to two or three phases that indicate movement or change connected with women and children. The family cannot go forward with ox-cart methods while other aspects of culture adopt more modern means of progress.

This matter of changing southern life will lead the study into a consideration of actual migrations. People have been moving out of the South in great numbers; a few have been coming in. More leaders and scholars have been drawn away than have been attracted to the region. How can this be explained? There must be reasons why southern-born ability goes rather than stays. People of all kinds, rich and poor, white and black, have also been moving out. This sort of change from place to place may be referred to as horizontal movement, and it means much in leadership, men, and money.

Another condition or aspect of change has to do with upgrade and downgrade patterns of interest and behavior. This might be termed vertical tendency or movement. Literature and scholarship, interest in them and production of them, may be looked upon as upgrade in contrast with crime and toleration of conditions that encourage it which are inevitably downgrade. Dr. Odum has pointed out that in the hundreds of special measures of condition which have been catalogued, more of them have been downgrade deficiency and waste than have been upgrade efficiency and thrift; more that makes for destruction than for construction and enrichment of life. The study of the moment will, then, take special note of the southern record in literature and crime, strange bookfellows that they be!

Is it possible that the type and patterning of family life as these feed other basic social institutions—school, church, community, and government

—may indicate some explanations as to why scholars and others leave home; as to why learning and literature have been scarce while ignorance and crime have been notorious aspects of southern culture? Can this be said of any race or region: Improve the family life of the people and you will lift the entire culture level, for the culture of a people cannot rise higher than its family life makes possible?

A. Aims for the student
1. To examine a few aspects of the southern family as an indicative and influential part of total southern culture.
2. To learn something of the meaning of population change in the South, both as to quality and quantity.
3. To sample certain downgrade actualities and upgrade possibilities connected with the region's crime record.
4. To sample the upgrade actualities and promise of southern literature in view of the heavy loss of native leadership to other regions.

B. Reading material for study
Southern Regions, Chapter I, pp. 149-153; Chapter IX, pp. 495-501. (Review pp. 481-487.) (Correction: in the first printing, page 497, the nineteenth line, the fourth word should be "remediable.")

Suggested additional reading: *Culture in the South*, Chapters VIII, IX, X, XIV, XXIV, and XXV.

C. Definitions and general guidance
Institutions rest on ideas and crystallized customs or *mores* that have been found good by long usage and that are indispensable to human welfare. A social institution is built upon some idea or ideas involving purpose, control, permanence, authority, and specific leadership and participation. Hence the home, school, church, state, etc., are social institutions. Or, to put it another way, an institution is an idea plus a structure, for example the family and the home, education and the school, religion and the church, law and order and the state, humanitarianism and a system of social welfare, and so on. Thus, like the word "culture" which, properly used, is not limited to refinement, "institution" means far more than a brick building with inmates.

Chronological strata: This term refers to periods such as the colonial, the slavery, the war, the reconstruction, the industrial, etc. It may also suggest quality of time as Europe with its Dark Age, Middle Age, Rebirth, Enlightenment, Industrial Revolution, etc. Like the stratification of rocks,

ASPECTS OF GENERAL CULTURE

time strata may have both quantity and quality. The time quantity of the World War was slight; its time quality or intensity was enormous.

Extractive occupations: Farming, mining, etc.

Distributive and social occupations: Clerical, selling, secretarial, teaching, ministerial, social work, etc.

Stereotype literally means a mold which reproduces copies exactly like the original, hence any saying that is applied automatically is referred to as a stereotype. Here are some: "All Negroes steal"; "poor but honest"; "terrible Turk"; and 1900 years ago: "Can any good thing come out of Nazareth?"

D. Questions primarily on facts and mapograph interpretations

1. List some stereotypes of the South; the North; the West. Of what real descriptive value are they and how reliable?
2. It is said that the South will have to be understood more realistically than through stereotypes and stage characterizations. What harm, if any, is there in so many songs and plays about southern moons and maids, rivers and boats, cotton fields and tobacco roads, and chivalry and romance amid pillared mansions and magnolia blossoms?
3. What is the substance of meaning in the reference to Councils, Conferences, and periodicals as mentioned on page 149?
4. What explanation can be ventured for this: The drain of leadership out of the South is "least with the historians, greater among the economists, psychologists, and political scientists, and quite high among sociologists, anthropologists, and statisticians?" Do southerners favor certain types of research and knowledge while they hold other types in disfavor? (Is truth ever to be feared?)
5. In the chart on page 148 is there any significant change to be noted for the two periods in the Southeast and in the Northeast?
6. Are Negroes moving horizontally, that is, from one area to another (pp. 88, 89, and 477)? Why? Are they on the upward move, that is, vertically from low levels of living to high (pp. 483-487)?
7. How can the criminal record of the South be explained? (No single answer can be given, certainly not one on the basis of race since the Negro has increasingly been showing a favorable record.) What ought to be done about it? What can be done? What will be done?
8. Are farm life and reliance on the Bible likely to make for families where the father is in high control (patriarchal) or are these likely to promote equality between all members including children? Why?
9. In what ways has the South emphasized the family as the foundation of human society? Illustrate.
10. What region has the most employed women in extractive occupations? In

distributive and social occupations? (Maps and chart, p. 500.) Are there any special implications?
11. After referring to the two maps on the upper half of page 498, offer an explanation as to why there is a high percentage of southern employed children in one instance and not in the other. In what pursuits, then, does most of the child labor occur?
12. Can it be said that the Southeast still reflects much of the culture pattern of earlier America?

E. Questions primarily on policy and program
1. The South has quantities of children and a high birth rate. Should more emphasis be placed on quality and a lower birth rate? What part should the state, the community, the church, and the family take in a "quality" program?
2. Why does the book say on page 501: "Child labor was logical"? Is it logical today and will it be so tomorrow? Discuss.
3. What evidence is there that the South will do great things in literature and drama in the years just ahead?
4. Why is it futile to analyze and direct southern regional politics without understanding and directing its farm and school folkways and tendencies?

F. Topics for debate and forum
1. Southern children should stay in school longer and marry later.
2. Nine out of ten native southerners who achieve distinction receive their awards after they have left the South; therefore, the South cannot give what is necessary to keep leadership in the region.
3. The Negro is the explanation of southern liabilities.
4. Negroes should be encouraged to leave rather than to remain in the South.

UNIT XX

SUBREGIONS OF THE SOUTHEAST

Be it emphasized again, that from the standpoint of culture there is no longer *a* South, but *many* Souths.

"The Solid South," a term born of political strife, is often thought to apply to all other aspects of southern life. But on close examination this popular expression is found to be not only inaccurate, but actually misleading. Even in the field of its birth, politics, it is somewhat doubtful if it truly reflects the present condition; as many persons discovered to their amazement in 1928.

This is not to deny that there is southernness as pictured in the book and study up to this point. Undoubtedly there is what may be considered a southern region; or better, there is a Southeast and a Southwest. The evidence of distinctiveness of the eleven states forming the southeastern portion of the nation is conclusive and undeniable.

However, when the investigator ceases to look at the Southeast as a whole and to compare it with the rest of the nation; and, instead, begins the closer study of the components of the region, wide differences between states and other portions of the greater region come into view. That is, the Southeast, or any other region, has a sameness throughout, a general pattern of life organization which distinguishes it from the remainder of the nation. But within that general pattern are smaller patterns which are distinctive within themselves. As an illustration, if we imagine the Southeast as a landscape painting of one general theme, we nevertheless also see various shades and blocks of color of distinctive hues which are combined into the larger composition. These distinctive blocks are the subregions.

This, of course, brings up the question of whether or not we should combine differing areas and lump them together as one region. Perhaps the best answer to this question lies in the *degree* of difference between the parts. In general, it may be said, the various parts of a true region in the sense in which the term is used by social science, differ less as among themselves than the region they form differs from other regions formed by similar subregions. That is, they must fit together so as to produce a relatively harmonious composition. Also, since the region must be large enough to contain a fairly complete cross section of social life, it needs different portions; mountains as well as plains, farming as well as manufacturing; Republicans as well as Democrats; Catholics as well as Protestants. It is in examining these minor differences that the subregional analysis becomes essential.

The question, in the end, resolves itself into one of the degrees of homogeneity desired. The eleven southeastern states are homogeneous, when viewed from the standpoint of the nation as a whole. There are various areas within this region which are still more homogeneous and may be taken as subregions. But even within these subregions, differences, heterogeneities, still exist, so that the process of subdivision may be carried on as far as may be desirable for any given purpose—even down to individual and personal differences. Obviously, of course, too much subdivision defeats its own purpose when the unit is made too small to have social meaning or to be used for social planning.

Too, the size and shape of the subregion defined will vary with the basis upon which the division is made. Thus we may have subregions based on geographic, economic, social, religious, urban, or any number of other considerations. It is also to be noted that these subregions will often overlap. Thus, the urban region of Atlanta includes mountain, piedmont, and plain, overlapping three geographic subregions. In general, subregions can be marked out in terms of (1) geography, demography, or population factors; or (2) as to the way they use their powers and resources; or (3) in social terms of opinion, attitude, and behavior. Usually the three factors are more or less interdependent so that the subregion defined in terms of one of these factors also fits roughly that defined in terms of either or both of the others. The metropolitan or urban region, which is often said to be overlaid on the others, perhaps cuts across the boundaries laid out by geography, function, and social organization more than any other form of organization.

A. Aims for the student
1. To gain a clearer insight into the methods used by painstaking social scientists in outlining regions and subregions.
2. To get an idea of the relativity of the regional concepts; to see the region as *relatively*, rather than *absolutely*, distinct from surrounding areas.
3. More specifically, to investigate the important differences which actually exist in a region often thought of as being very much alike throughout its parts.
4. To realize the importance of the subregion to an understanding of or planning for a large region.

B. Reading material for study
Southern Regions, Chapter I, pp. 153-163; Chapter III, pp. 277-290. The index of *Southern Regions* may be used to advantage for further reading on the subject.

Suggested additional reading: *Human Geography of the South*, Chapters II, VII-XII. *Preface to Peasantry*, Chapters I, II, VI-IX.

Treat as review any overlapping or duplication of reading material with earlier units.

C. Definitions and general guidance

Homogeneity; Heterogeneity: These terms as used by Dr. Odum carry very much of the ordinary dictionary meanings. An area is homogeneous when its parts are similar, heterogeneous when they are different. Similarity and difference are, however, terms which take their meaning from the point of view of the person using them; that is, they are relative. To most persons living outside the South, all Negroes look alike; just as all Chinese look alike to most Americans. From the view of the outsider, Negroes and Chinese form highly homogeneous groups. But from the point of view of those insiders who know these peoples intimately, they are heterogeneous; decided differences are recognized and taken as a matter of course—as between Negro school teachers and farm hands, or those of Virginia and those of Mississippi. Just so, those who have resided in the Orient know that there is a great difference between the Chinese in the northern and southern portions of that great nation. Thus the Southeast is at once homogeneous and heterogeneous, depending on the point of view of the observer.

Black Belt: (People) Stretching from North Carolina through South Carolina, Georgia, Alabama, and into Mississippi is an area in the form of a rough crescent in which more than half the population is Negro. Here are found the richest soil and the poorest people. This subregion of the Southeast is known as the "Black Belt," because of this predominance of black folk. (In the Southwest the term refers also to the black waxy soil.) Here we have an illustration of a demographic region. It should be noted that the functional division would place this area within the cotton area and thereby identify it with the other cotton-producing subregions as marked out by T. J. Woofter, Jr. But a cotton-producing area in which most of the inhabitants are Negroes is somewhat different in social organization from one in which the workmen are white; hence, it was deemed advisable to distinguish the two. In terms of use, the Black Belt is a variant of the Cotton Belt; in terms of population it is quite different. (See Unit XXIII.)

Marginal land and marginal folk: Economists define marginal land as that land which produces only enough to repay the cultivator for the actual expenses of cultivation, including wages at the customary level. In theory, it is assumed that if a person can make more money at some other work, he will quit his present job and take the one offering higher returns. The point at which he would thus transfer from one sort of work to another is called the "margin." Actually, other factors keep this transfer from taking place readily, and we have many persons in the Southeast remaining on farms which do not return the actual cost of cultivation when that cost is estimated by any accounting which would be acceptable in modern business. These lands and the people occupying them are then marginal or submarginal; that is, they exist at or below the no-profit point. The explanation of this is far too complex to be entered here, but it may be said that tradition and ignorance are two of the powerful factors producing the condition. In the study quoted, the margin has been placed at the point of $22.50 value per acre of land and buildings. This seems to be a fair figure, though the margin will shift with the operation of other forces which raise or lower prices in general.

Socio-economic entity: This term refers to areas which have a definite and distinctive social and economic organization. Illustrations are the Birmingham iron mining and smelting district, the Louisiana "Sugar Bowl," or the city of Charleston, South Carolina. There is a tendency to read into this term a meaning of self-sufficiency which it does not have. Such areas are dependent upon other areas, often to a greater degree than the region as a whole, because of their intense specialization, which forces them to secure a larger proportion of the things consumed from other areas. The term is largely synonymous with "subregion," though it may be used to refer to either a larger or smaller area than is described as a subregion in this study.

It should be remembered that the subregion is very similar to the region, and therefore most of the discussion of regions will also apply to the subregion, with due allowance for differences in size and homogeneity.

D. **Questions primarily on facts and mapograph interpretations**
   1. Note the fourteen basic indices used to measure the homogeneity of the southeastern states. List these indices in what appears to you to be their order of importance. Can you think of other measurable indices which you think essential?
   2. Why is it impossible to understand or to plan for a large region from a description made up in terms of averages?
   3. What sort of picture of life within the areas can you build up from the tables on pages 158 and 226? What other figures would you like to have to complete your picture?
   4. Why does the Southwest have a better chance to escape damage from erosion than has the Southeast? (See page 185.)
   5. Why do you suppose Dr. Odum gives figures showing both the value of land

SUBREGIONS OF THE SOUTHEAST

and buildings per acre and per farm? What other figures are needed to make these two comparable?

6. Compare the map of submarginal counties in the Southeast, on page 160, with that of subregions of the Southeast, on page 158. Do you find a definite connection between types of use and submarginal conditions? If so, which is cause and which is effect?
7. Outline the geographic factors seen as important in delimiting the subregions of the Southeast. How important do geographic factors appear to be in outlining subregions?
8. Repeat the directions in question 7 for some other subregion of the nation— the Great Plains or New England, for example—and then check your conclusion as to the value of geographic factors in determining subregions.
9. Is the dominance of one crop a sufficient reason for determining a subregion? For instance, should all cotton-growing areas be placed in one category?
10. Should the entire Southern Appalachian district be classified as one subregion? Should the entire Appalachian mountain area be classified as one region? Why or why not?
11. Compare the size of the subregions of the Southeast with those of the Southwest. What is the basis of this difference?
12. What objections occur to you to making subregions very small?
13. Does the existence of two or more agricultural experiment stations in each state support the argument for the existence of subregions within these states?
14. Compare the map of river basins, on page 162, with one of the subregional maps of the Southeast. What does this indicate as to the value of using river basins as subregions? As to the use of rivers as boundary lines?
15. What do the map and chart on page 152 indicate as to the importance of demographic factors in delimiting subregions? What factors might be used to explain the changes shown there?

E. Questions primarily on policy and program
  1. From the discussion of question D-15 above, and your general knowledge of the situation within these various subregions, outline a plan which you think would bring about a better population distribution.
  2. Compare the criteria used in subdividing the Southeast and the Southwest. How do you account for the differences? For instance, why is transportation of more importance in the Southwest?
  3. How do you explain the varying number and shape of the subregions of the Southeast by various scholars? Can all of these divisions be valid? Would the national government be likely to insist upon full agreement of experts before setting up subregional programs?
  4. The book says that Charleston and New Orleans "may be characterized as

distinctive subregional phenomena." Would this statement apply equally as well to Richmond and Atlanta? Why, or why not?
5. Some social scientists outline metropolitan regions in terms of wholesale trading areas, newspaper circulation, banking services, and similar functions. How would such areas fit in with the subregions mapped in this section? Would the metropolitan area illustrate a socio-economic entity?
6. Which of the various subregional schemes outlined on pages 159-161 do you think most valuable for use in planning better land utilization?
7. From the table on page 158 divide the Southeast into tenancy subregions and then compare your results with other subregional divisions. What does this suggest as to remedial measures?
8. How do you account for the Republican political subregion found in the Southern Appalachians? What is the cultural significance of this area?
9. The subregion of lowest value in the Southeast is found in southern Georgia and northern Florida. Discuss causes and possible remedial measures for this situation.

F. Topics for debate and forum
1. Debate the statement, "Florida is not a true southern state." (Maryland, West Virginia, Texas, furnish other examples of states in a similarly debatable status, and might be used in place of Florida.)
2. From a study of maps of subregions, and from other considerations, discuss the validity of using state lines as regional and subregional boundaries.
3. Discuss the rôle of tradition in preserving functional subregional divisions. (The cotton-growing tradition in the South, for example.)
4. Debate the statement, "The fact that the Black Belt contains more than twice as many submarginal counties as any other southeastern subregion indicates that Negroes are incapable of attaining or acquiring a high economic and cultural level."

NOTES

NOTES

SUBREGIONS OF THE SOUTHWEST

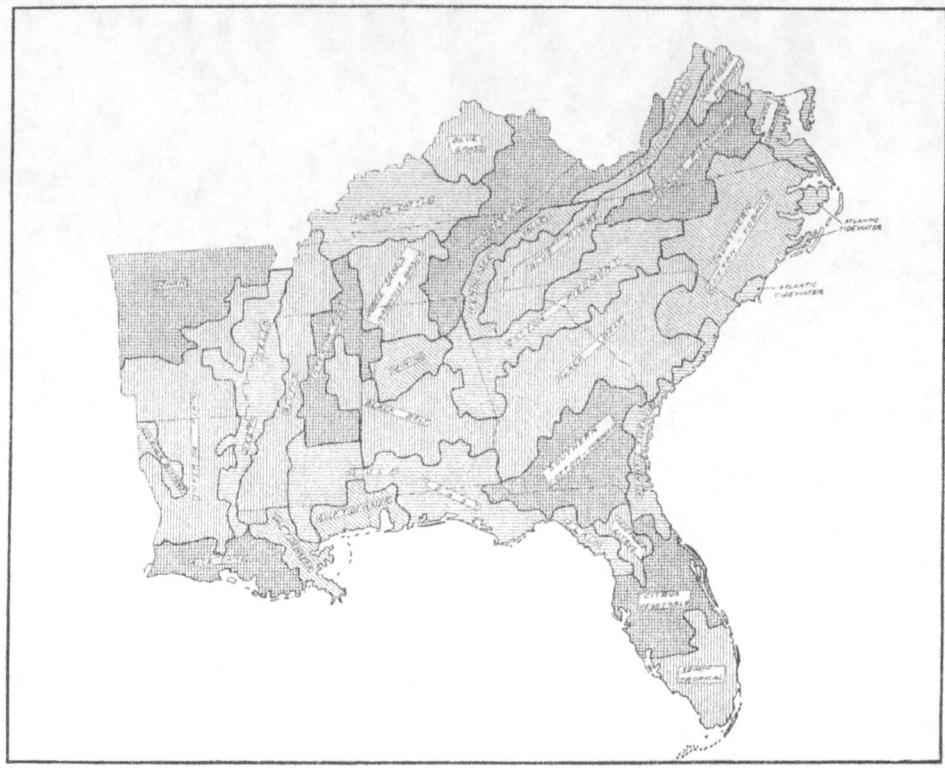

COUNTY MEDIANS OF SELECTED INDICES OF THE SUBREGIONS IN THE SOUTHERN REGION OF THE UNITED STATES: AGRICULTURE

SUBREGION	Per Cent Tenancy	Per Cent White Tenancy	Per Cent Negro Tenancy	Per Cent Land in Farms	Average Size Farms (Acres)	Value Land and Buildings Per Farm	Value Land and Buildings Per Acre
Cotton Piedmont	63.9	55.5	85.1	71.9	65.1	$2,269	$36
Shenandoah Valley	16.6	17.0	12.5	65.3	110.4	7,728	74
Tennessee Valley	37.2	37.0	43.4	78.7	79.6	3,556	37
Atlantic Tidewater	18.5	19.2	18.5	37.6	79.3	3,823	47
Northern Piedmont	15.4	16.0	12.5	75.5	129.8	7,997	54
Tobacco Piedmont	31.5	26.9	41.0	70.0	92.6	3,105	34
Blue Ridge Mountains	30.9	30.0	23.1*	53.1	76.8	2,420	35
Cumberland Mountains	28.7	28.7	12.1	64.0	79.0	2,199	27
Blue Grass	41.0	40.7	44.5	88.5	79.7	5,137	71
Tobacco-Cattle	38.8	37.6	50.9	81.3	83.4	2,354	27
Muscle Shoals-Nashville Basin	44.2	43.9	57.1	74.5	80.4	2,747	41
Bluffs	74.7	51.4	86.6	69.0	65.8	1,627	26
Northern Cotton and Tobacco	58.3	47.5	73.5	58.2	61.5	2,775	43
Southern Cotton and Tobacco	60.4	55.0	71.6	58.0	104.5	2,479	24
Black Belt	73.5	49.4	88.3	58.3	79.9	1,875	24
Citrus-Vegetable	8.6	10.0	25.0	8.7	51.3	14,703	205
Vegetable-Citrus	30.1	29.9	28.8	30.9	100.0	3,720	41
Semi-Tropical	34.9	32.6	75.0	3.1	43.2	7,532	156
Gulf Coast Plain	41.7	34.0	55.7	36.6	76.3	2,012	25
Mining	50.8	49.6	63.9	49.4	64.8	1,859	26
Gulf Tidewater	25.2	24.3	43.6	15.4	72.5	3,824	53
Interior Ridge	57.0	48.6	71.7	70.7	70.9	1,398	19
Delta	90.3	75.5	95.3	50.6	34.5	2,271	57
Ozarks	42.7	42.6	46.2*	53.3	89.7	2,092	25
Interior Plain	61.2	49.3	79.1	39.0	60.8	1,875	31
Red River Bottoms	80.0	54.5	89.0	43.2	41.8	2,015	48
Rice-Cane	51.9	42.1	67.8	33.7	138.9	7,004	49

*More than 10 per cent of counties with no Negro tenancy.

Reprinted from page 158 in *Southern Regions*.

UNIT XXI

THE TENNESSEE VALLEY

PERHAPS NO other governmental activity of the 1930's has created more discussion than the attempts to apply social planning to the Tennessee River Valley. In several quarters there has been more excitement about it than calm study and appraisal of what was attempted, or of what has been accomplished. To many, such an activity on the part of the government is an indication that socialism, communism, anarchism, or some other terrible "ism" has not only gained a foothold in our nation, but has received official sanction. Others, equally sincere, hail the Tennessee Valley Authority as a great step toward a higher and better life which can be attained only through the action of the agency of all the people, the government. In either case the viewpoint of social science is missed for the efforts of the TVA, as it is called, afford an exceptionally valuable opportunity to watch the forces of social change actually at work.

The Tennessee Valley Authority may be viewed as conducting a huge social experiment which may or may not be valuable in developing a particular area of the nation, but which is certainly of great value insofar as it throws light upon the question of whether or not such schemes can be made to work, whether they should be made to work, and if so, how they can be operated most effectively. From this point of view the actual concrete results of the experiment are not so important as the opportunity afforded to study the value and means of bringing about social change on a large scale.

The Tennessee Valley is a sort of social science laboratory. All of the social sciences have much to learn from it, but the whole experiment is especially suggestive to the person interested in regionalism because the valley is a sizeable subregion. Hence, what is proven true or false in this experiment will indicate, to a greater or lesser degree, what may be expected to take place in other regions under conditions more or less similar to those found here.

Thus, the Tennessee Valley becomes of national and even of international importance. The President has called it a "yardstick" with which to measure production techniques, use, social importance, and rates of electric power. But it is also a "yardstick" with which the whole idea of regionalism and of social planning may be gauged. This is especially true in reference to the southeastern region of the United States, since in many ways the Tennessee Valley is a true sample of the larger region of which it is a part. Conditions within this smaller area do not exactly duplicate those of the Southeast as a whole, of course, but they are similar enough so that what is true of the valley is highly indicative of what is true of the entire region. In slightly less degree the same statement may be applied to the whole nation. So that we might say, borrowing a term from politics, "As goes Tennessee Valley, so may go the nation."

In addition to these prospects and values the development of a large area of the nation is in itself a most important undertaking. Portions of the Tennessee Valley are included within an area which has attracted a great deal of discussion, thought, and even pity. Being less developed than surrounding areas, lying near enough to large cities and highly developed sections to be easily accessible, it has attracted the attention of the eastern portion of the nation. Both students and philanthropists have earned excellent dividends on their investments of time and funds in their efforts to understand and to reform. For these reasons such a program in this area is better understood and, therefore, has more importance than if undertaken in a more remote portion of the nation.

Since the Tennessee Valley project is under way at this writing, and since its accomplishments are not yet subject to final judgment, it is imperative that the student look into the most recent literature available before he forms an opinion as to the value of the program as a means of aiding the region. This is slightly less important for study of the experiment from the theoretical point of view, but since theory is valuable only if it actually explains or guides, it is apparent that current happenings in the subregion are essential here also. Unfortunately any published work, a book especially, cannot show the situation at the moment. As this is written, the portrayal in *Southern Regions* is accurate, but before this appears in print something may have happened to change the situation greatly. Hence the necessity of the latest available information.

A. **Aims for the student**
   1. To gain an insight into the problem of regional analysis through consideration of a concrete illustration.
   2. To discover some of the actual problems of social planning through a discussion of those found within a given region.
   3. To observe how a subregion may be representative of the larger region of which it is a part.

4. To note the interrelationships of one area with another.
5. To test some of the ideas he has formed concerning regions and regionalism by applying them to a specific problem.

B. Reading material for study
Southern Regions, Chapter I, pp. 163-173; Chapter VII, pp. 453-455.

Suggested additional reading: *Human Geography of the South*, Chapter II, pp. 34-37; Chapter X. *Culture in the South*, Chapter XIX.

There is a vast amount of recent periodical literature describing one or more phases of the Tennessee Valley experiment. The files of popular high class magazines for the past three years will give the student more material than he can find time to read. The Tennessee Valley Authority has published several studies and will publish others. The National Resources Committee has an excellent study of the valley in its volume *Regional Factors in National Development*.

C. Definitions and general guidance
National-regional experiment: One of the greatest differences between the social and "natural" sciences has been the lack of experimentation in the former. The social scientist has been forced to observe what has actually happened rather than arrange to apply forces, incidence, and then observe the results. The Tennessee Valley, a national-regional project, along with other "New Deal" projects, partly removes this disability. The word order is important, since it reflects the philosophy of regionalism as developed by Howard W. Odum. In his view, the nation always comes first, the region second. This is what distinguishes his eyes-front *regionalism* from the older, longing-look-over-the-shoulder *sectionalism*.

Cross fertilization: This is a term borrowed from botany, and has much the same meaning in social science that it has in natural science. Social characteristics of one region are mixed with those of another, and the result is often that a new form appears. Historic examples are numerous and important. For instance, when the Chinese art of printing was cross-fertilized with the Phoenician alphabet, the publishing industry sprang into being with all its great power for changing ways of life. In the world of ideas, it can be argued that man is fully capable of improving on nature in his social arrangements. Ideas can be improved, even as fruit and flowers, by crossing. Cross fertilization of science with humanitarian and democratic ideas is behind the movement for social planning. (See Chapter III, *inbreeding*.)

Agricultural-industrial equilibrium: Both agriculture and industry are necessary to the best possible social system in this country. For some decades industry has been making rapid advance while agriculture, though also making very important advances, has become of less importance relatively. Within the past few years two things have happened which have caused many social thinkers to believe that agriculture must be given more importance, must be brought back into better balance with industry. The depression following the collapse of 1929 seems to have demonstrated that industry, at least as now operating, cannot take care of great masses of people in time of crisis and that an over-industrialized society would be in serious danger from economic forces not wholly understood and certainly not well controlled. The second factor is the way in which industry is turning more and more to products of the farm for its raw materials—the movement known as *chemurgy*. This means much greater interdependence of agriculture and manufacturing and would seem to depend for success on a definite balancing of the two general means of producing wealth.

D. Questions primarily on facts and mapograph interpretations

1. Note the directions in which the Tennessee River flows and the states through which it passes. What is the heart of the TVA program as it has developed thus far? Is it physical or social in nature, or both?
2. How much money do engineers estimate might well be spent in construction of dams in the Southeast?
3. What is the three-fold significance of the Tennessee Valley program?
4. What are the definite goals, the primary objectives of the TVA? How do you account for the great diversity of opinion as to the worth of the Tennessee Valley program?
5. What states are included in the Tennessee Valley program? Are other states nearby as vitally affected?
6. What was the first town to receive power from the Tennessee Valley Authority? What important cities might use this power?
7. From a study of the map on page 168, does it appear to be true that the Tennessee Valley project will affect areas fairly well representative of the nation as a whole?
8. Make a list of the distinctive features of the Tennessee Valley. Does the diversity so shown add to or detract from its value as a national-regional experiment?
9. From a study of the table on page 170, how typical is the Tennessee Valley of the agricultural situation of the Southeast? Of the nation?
10. From the list of resources and materials on pages 453-455, make a list of possible industries which might operate in the Tennessee Valley. What effect would the establishment of such industries have on existing industrial arrangements?

11. List the trades and professions which are likely to be affected by the Tennessee Valley project.
12. How well, in your opinion, does the Tennessee Valley meet the requirements of an experimental area as set forth by Dr. Harcourt A. Morgan?
13. Discuss the human resources found within the Tennessee Valley area.
14. How well does the Tennessee Valley meet the five-fold test of regional analysis as outlined by Dr. Odum?
15. What fundamental issue concerning public utilities is directly concerned in the success or failure of the Tennessee Valley project? In what other programs of the government within recent times has this same issue appeared? How was it met in these other instances?

E. Questions primarily on policy and program
1. What are the implications of the Tennessee Valley program as to the efficiency of state political units?
2. Discuss the Tennessee Valley project as a means of bringing about better feelings between the various regions of the nation.
3. In its industrial development, should the Tennessee Valley seek old or new industries? That is, should it rely on the development of new processes to be used in its industries, or should it invite old industries, to which it can offer advantages, to change their location?
4. Discuss the development of the Tennessee Valley from the point of view of its influence on migration within the nation. Assuming an influx of population, what effect would that have on the general cultural level of the area?
5. Discuss the probable effect of development in the Tennessee Valley on the culture of surrounding states.
6. Assuming that the Tennessee Valley Authority fails to attain its objectives, does this mean the experiment is without value?
7. How does the Tennessee Valley experiment illustrate the problems of a change of technology and its effects upon a social system?
8. In what ways might the Tennessee Valley program affect the situation of Negroes in the South in general?

F. Topics for debate and forum
1. Debate the Tennessee Valley plan as a fair test of regionalism in the United States.
2. Debate the implications of the statement "a river (Tennessee) basin draining seven states, an authority draining forty-eight states."
3. Debate the river valley as the most suitable unit for development such as that undertaken by Tennessee Valley Authority.
4. Should there be created a regional advisory board composed of representatives of the states affected by the Tennessee Valley program to aid the Federal

Authority now operating the project? If so, what states would be entitled to representation?

5. Discuss possible effects of the Tennessee Valley development changing the relative importance of the area east of the Appalachian Mountains and the Mississippi Valley.

UNIT XXII

STATES AND REGIONS

SINCE THE state is a governmental unit, the study of the relations of regions and states necessarily takes us into the realm of politics. We must pay some attention to the manner in which state boundaries coincide with regional limits or fail to do so. On this point, what does the Tennessee Valley area suggest? We must advance the question of how well regions may be made up of groups of states. And this will lead us into some discussion of the possible value of regional forms of government as alternatives to some of the present duties of the states. Would it be possible to have United Regions of America?

This last question, of course, raises the much larger question of the centralization or decentralization of the national government and possible means to avoid too much of either of these tendencies. Certainly for the last century, the trend has been for the national government to take over more and more of the functions formerly performed by the states. The question the American people must face and answer within the next two or three decades, during the lifetime of those now in schools, is whether this tendency is good or bad, whether it should be encouraged or checked, or whether there may not be some other form of balance between federal and state governments which will be of greater advantage to the people of the nation as a whole. Some political scientists think a good alternative would be the creation of regional units of government. As a matter of fact, many of the duties of the federal government are now carried out through regional agencies, some of which serve areas smaller than one state, but most of which operate over a region composed of several states.

But the states are fortified in their present position by sentiments and social habits of more than a century's standing. They have been governmental units for a long time, and to change now would destroy many of our ideas, would upset our traditions, would leave some of our dearest loyalties without an object, and, in the opinion of many, would not be more efficient. So, there are arguments on both sides which need careful study and evaluation.

But the states have another value to the regionalist or to the student of a given region. Roughly, the regions are composed of states. Hence, if one wishes to discover the characteristics of a region it would be well to begin by seeking the characteristics of the states of which the region is composed. And it is very much easier to characterize a state than a region. This is true because the state has been a concrete object which has attracted loyalty and veneration as well as ridicule, because it has entered into the lives of the people of the nation. We have talked about states because we have thought in terms of states. And thinking and talking in terms of states has built up a mass of opinions about states, in the abstract and in concrete cases.

Beyond this states have been given nicknames which show in a rough sort of way the general opinion of the state and its inhabitants. The states have elected certain persons to public offices which have brought them into the public eye, where they have been assumed to be representative of the state. The states have chosen official mottoes, flowers, and other emblems which reflect the nature of the inhabitants more or less accurately. Even certain foods have become associated in popular thinking with certain states, as the codfish with Massachusetts. All of these things aid us in gaining an insight into the unmeasurable but highly important characteristics of the people who live in certain places.

When measurable characteristics are examined, figures are available for states, but not for regions, save in such arbitrarily chosen regions as those used by the Census Bureau. Thus, in the population composition, illiteracy, sums spent for schools, church membership, banking transactions, and so on throughout the long list of things measured and noted, the state is used as the unit. This is true because these figures are most commonly compiled by the government which naturally uses governmental units. So that as a matter of practicability, the student of a region is almost compelled to outline his region so as to have its boundaries coincide with state lines, whether he wishes to do so or not. Actually, he often does not wish to do so. Thus, in the case of the southeastern region, it is evident to all who have visited the area that the pine forested country in the eastern portion of Texas is very similar to the pine forested region extending from there through Virginia. Logically, therefore, the eastern portion of Texas should be included within the southeastern region on the evidence of this pine tree index and many other indices. But, since it is practically impossible to separate the figures of this portion of Texas from the remainder of the state, and the remainder of the state is by far the larger part, the entire state has been placed in the southwestern region.

For all of these reasons, the pictures of the states become an essential part of the picture of the region.

STATES AND REGIONS

A. Aims for the student
  1. To consider the significance of state governmental units in our modern political organization.
  2. To gain an understanding of the way in which the states combine to form a regional pattern.
  3. More specifically, to gain an insight into the characteristics of the states which form the southeastern region.
  4. Through the use of statistics by states, to compare and contrast conditions in the Southeast with those in other regions of the nation.

B. Reading material for study
  Southern Regions, Chapter I, pp. 173-179; Chapter X.

  Suggested additional reading: If copies are available, the student is also urged to read the report of the National Resources Committee, *Regional Factors in National Development*, and a little volume of lectures by C. E. Merriam, *The Written Constitution and the Unwritten Attitude*.

C. Definitions and general guidance
  State portraiture: A representation of the significant characteristics of a state, as a good portrait, shows the outstanding character of the subject. Neither the social scientist nor the painter can, or should, attempt to include every detail and produce a photographic likeness. The task of each is to present such details as give a true presentation, as accurately reflect the existing conditions. And, just as the painter shows many things he could not describe in terms of angles and lines, so the social scientist presents true impressions which cannot always be supported by neat tables and charts.

  Chronological lag: Often it is observed that one set of ideas, or the general condition of one portion of a nation, is in about the same position occupied by another set of ideas or portion of the nation at a definite time in the past and seems to be changing about as the other did. Hence, it is assumed that after the lapse of a certain time the backward factor will have arrived at the present position of the more advanced. For instance, the Negro death rate is falling much after the manner of the white death rate of thirty to forty years ago. That is, there seems to be a chronological lag of some thirty or forty years in this situation. (See *cultural lag, time lag,* and *chronological strata* defined in earlier units.)

D. Questions primarily on facts and mapograph interpretations
  1. How wide a range of differences do you find between the various states of the southeastern region? Which are most typically southern?

2. What is the significance of per capita postal receipts in understanding the culture of a state or region?
3. How would you explain the low average amount of life insurance carried by persons living in the Southeast? Would the same explanation hold for New Mexico and Arizona?
4. What is the value of state differences and likenesses in depicting a regional social organization?
5. From the chart on pages 538 and 540, and the various other similar characterizations, how adequate a picture of the states can you secure?
6. Examine the lists on pages 552 and 554. How important are these superlatives like biggest, oldest, first, etc.? Do they balance the superlatives connected with education, libraries, health, crime, etc.? Of what value to the social scientists are state mottoes, favorite foods, nicknames, etc.?
7. List the better known political leaders of the Southeast against state nicknames, mottoes, favorite foods, etc. From the general reputation these men bear, how well do they represent the culture of their states?
8. From the professions represented by the leading men of the various southeastern states, what conclusion do you draw as to the cultural interests of the region?
9. From the maps on page 176, draw up a generalized picture of southern agriculture. From other maps and tables, found by use of the index, supplement this picture and check the accuracy of your first generalization.
10. Compare the ranks of southeastern states in public education, shown on the map on page 172, with the percentage of tax revenues required to meet the national average. What are the implications of this comparison?
11. What political folkways are to be read from the table, page 546, showing the composition of the legislative bodies of the various southeastern states? Do you think these men fairly representative of the states as a whole?
12. What is the value of state totals rather than state averages in comparisons of states of different regions?
13. What is the explanation of the paradox of North Carolina, low in averages and high in aggregates, and Nevada, high in averages and low in aggregates?
14. How do you explain the fact that Florida, the southeastern state at the greatest distance from other regions, is the least typical of its region?
15. How do you explain the great number of state organizations now in existence? How many of them grew out of the state as a political unit? How many of them could be reorganized on a regional basis to better advantage?

E. **Questions primarily on policy and program**
1. How do the coastal trucking fringe, the rice belt, the tobacco belt, and the piney woods section complicate the problem of planning by state units? How could this problem be met?

2. What non-material factors make it difficult to change the existing forms of economic, political, or social activity? Do you have any suggestions as to how this situation might be changed?
3. Can you think of any exceptions to the statement of the National Resources Committee that a major development project probably will never fall wholly within state boundaries?
4. Does it appear likely that the people of the Southeast would look with favor upon the creation of regional governmental units to take over part of the functions now performed by the states? Why?
5. How do you explain the steady increase in the power of the federal government? Is this good or bad? Why?
6. Outline several problems which neither the state nor federal governments appears able to handle satisfactorily. Would regional administrative units meet these situations more effectively?
7. Discuss the position of the "Middle South" as the core of the southeastern region. How do you explain the relative divergence of the other states of the Southeast?

F. Topics for debate and forum
1. Our states are historical accidents and now constitute a national dilemma.
2. Anything, particularly the state, that has great traditions should be preserved.
3. Local loyalty and pride are nearer to the interests of the average person; therefore, instead of fewer states, we should have more states.
4. Nevada ranks higher in civilization and culture than North Carolina. North Dakota outranks Virginia. Support your arguments with figures and historical illustrations.
5. State planning boards rather than regional planning boards are sufficient for present needs.
6. "The leaders are of, by, and for the states."

NOTES

Subregions of the Southwest

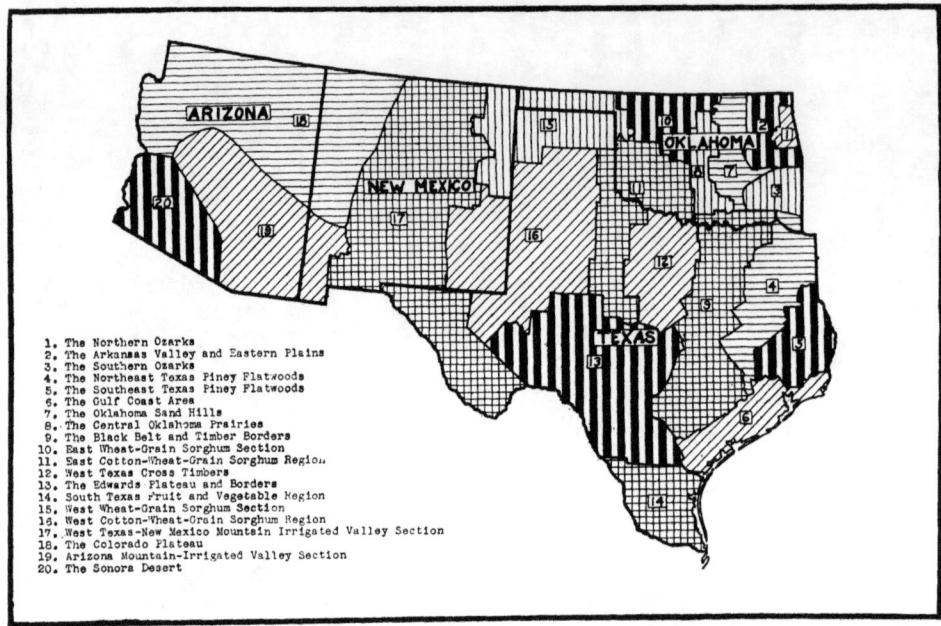

1. The Northern Ozarks
2. The Arkansas Valley and Eastern Plains
3. The Southern Ozarks
4. The Northeast Texas Piney Flatwoods
5. The Southeast Texas Piney Flatwoods
6. The Gulf Coast Area
7. The Oklahoma Sand Hills
8. The Central Oklahoma Prairies
9. The Black Belt and Timber Borders
10. East Wheat-Grain Sorghum Section
11. East Cotton-Wheat-Grain Sorghum Region
12. West Texas Cross Timbers
13. The Edwards Plateau and Borders
14. South Texas Fruit and Vegetable Region
15. West Wheat-Grain Sorghum Section
16. West Cotton-Wheat-Grain Sorghum Region
17. West Texas-New Mexico Mountain Irrigated Valley Section
18. The Colorado Plateau
19. Arizona Mountain-Irrigated Valley Section
20. The Sonora Desert

These subregions, analogous to those represented by Woofter for the Southeast, were designated as tentative subdivisions by Raymond Thomas. They are discussed at length by him in his special study of the Southwest. See Thomas' special viewpoint on subregions and state lines in Chapter X.

Population and Area of Subregions of the Southwest

REGION	Area in Sq. Mi.	Population	Urban Population	Rural Population	Population Per Sq. Mi.	Per Cent Urban	Per Cent Rural
No. 1	3,000	60,000		60,000	20.		100
No. 2	7,500	520,000	241,244	278,756	69.7	46.3	53.7
No. 3	5,743	86,928		86,928	15.1		100
No. 4	18,634	651,391	117,261	534,130	34.9	18.0	82.0
No. 5	14,025	284,111	23,929	260,182	20.2	8.4	91.6
No. 6	14,762	825,639	528,105	297,533	55.9	63.9	36.1
No. 7	9,963	454,175	133,653	320,522	45.5	29.4	70.6
No. 8	6,949	446,116	251,641	194,475	64.1	56.4	43.6
No. 9	37,782	2,245,563	1,039,764	1,205,799	59.4	46.3	53.7
No. 10	12,015	255,747	77,654	178,091	21.2	30.3	69.7
No. 11	27,855	665,570	160,064	505,506	23.9	24.0	76.0
No. 12	18,611	382,585	120,642	261,943	20.5	31.5	68.5
No. 13	53,317	283,326	74,336	208,990	5.3	26.2	73.8
No. 14	17,217	271,057	126,400	144,657	15.7	46.6	53.4
No. 15	28,800	133,109	30,047	103,062	4.6	22.5	77.5
No. 16	58,947	465,507	133,217	332,290	7.9	28.6	71.4
No. 17	83,691	405,781	183,119	222,662	4.8	45.1	54.9
No. 18	88,266	144,410	13,800	130,610	1.6	9.5	90.5
No. 19	37,960	370,753	140,675	230,078	9.7	37.9	62.1
No. 20	21,987	29,816	4,892	24,924	1.4	16.4	83.6
Total	567,024	8,981,584	3,400,443	5,581,138	15.8	37.8	62.2

Reprinted from page 186 in *Southern Regions*.

UNIT XXIII

THE SOUTHWEST AND THE SOUTHEAST

STATISTICS OF "The South" nearly always embrace Texas and Oklahoma, and often include Maryland and Missouri. On grounds of history and economics there is some justification for such a grouping. Slavery existed, although in a rather limited degree, in all four of the states. Some cotton is still produced in Missouri, while Texas and Oklahoma now produce almost half of the cotton of the nation. Slavery ceased to exist more than a half-century ago; cotton, although remaining one of the dominant factors in the lives of the people who produce it, is after all, only *one* factor. Hence, the question arises as to how "Southern" these states really are.

Southern Regions has already made it very clear by many measures that the culture of these four states is not the same as that of the states composing the southeastern region; that the people in these states live, act, and think much more like those to the north and west than to those to the south and east of them. The concrete evidence of the measurable indices is supported by the impression one gains of habits and opinions which cannot be gauged accurately, and both point to the conclusion that these states are different, that they do not fit into the general picture of the southeastern region.

Missouri as no longer South has been noted by most writers for some time; as for Maryland, the point has been debated; but in the case of Texas and Oklahoma it has been assumed by most students that here is a portion, or at least an extension, of "The South." Was not Texas a part of the Confederacy? Was it not settled mostly by persons from the old South? Does it not extend further south, geographically, than any other state save Florida? Is it not true that the civilized Indian tribes of Oklahoma supported the Confederacy? And that people from the southern states poured into that territory in a thin trickle until the Indian lands were opened to settlement, when that trickle became a raging torrent which quickly turned cattle ranges into cotton patches as restrictions were removed? Are they not both south of the Mason-Dixon line?

These things are true, and insofar as they determine the complexion of a region, Texas and Oklahoma are similar to the Southeast. But as shown earlier in this study there are many other indices which must be taken into account when one attempts to describe accurately a region; and these other indices bend these particular states out of the Southeast. Soil, climate, topography, growing season, vegetation, products of the farms, transportation systems, manufacturing, the place of the cities, education, religion, history and tradition, racial composition, and social conditions in general all establish the fact that here is a different people living in a different region.

Nor does this vast area fit into the general pattern of the Northwest or the Far West any better than it does into that of the Southeast. Take Kansas and Texas, for example—it is impossible to think of them as belonging together, just as it is impossible to think of Oklahoma and Louisiana as being part of the same region in spite of the fact that only a few miles separate the latter two states.

Hence the regionalist must recognize the existence of another region. But immediately the question arises as to how far west this area extends. Here we have New Mexico and Arizona, usually thought of as being part of the Far West, but upon closer examination showing such definite differences that to say that Arizona and California are alike is entirely unsupportable. But these states are much like the greater portions of Oklahoma and Texas in geography, population composition, history, and above all, in the spirit of the people. So, by a process of separation of unlikes and union of likes, the Southwest region forces itself into our division of the nation.

The Southwest and the Southeast have much in common; so much that together they might form *a* South if not *the* South of which we have grown accustomed to thinking. But they have many differences also; so many that they are distinctive regions with some trend toward unlikeness rather than likeness.

A. Aims for the student
1. To investigate the idea of "The South."
2. To illustrate the necessity of using many factors in outlining a region.
3. To show how the social scientist goes about the "discovery" of a region.
4. To point out some of the distinctions between the Southwest and the Southeast.

B. Reading material for study
Southern Regions, Chapter I, pp. 179-187.

Suggested additional reading: *Human Geography of the South,* Chapter XIII; *The Collapse of Cotton Tenancy,* Chapter III; although these two readings apply to earlier units, they may be reviewed here to advantage. Also, if available, *The Great Plains,* by Walter P. Webb, affords a fine description of life in the Great Plains area.

C. Definitions and general guidance

Economic nerves: For a century or more numerous philosophers and some social scientists have sought to explain the organization of society by comparing it to a human body. This method has the advantage of illustrating social processes in terms of biological processes easily understood by the elementary student. Thus the nerve system of the human body carries out the function of keeping the body as a whole informed of what is taking place in the various organs. Similarly, the paths along which commodities and news are carried keep the social body informed as to what is happening throughout the society. That is, trade and communication routes are somewhat similar to nerves. Thus, the economic nerves of a region would consist of the trade and communication routes of that region, the rail and waterways, the telephone and telegraph lines, etc.; all the means used to convey economic goods and information. Needless to say, the more complex the civilization, the more important these nerves.

Black Belt: (Soil) This term is used in two senses. In the older Southeast, it commonly refers to districts in which more than half the population is Negro. But in the Southwest, the term indicates a strip of black, waxy soil of great fertility which extends from near the Red River in northeastern Texas in a southwesterly direction almost to the Rio Grande near Laredo, Texas. Because of its superior fertility, this strip of soil has been important in the development of the entire state of Texas. There is a similar strip of soil in Alabama which is also spoken of as a "Black Belt." In the discussion of the Southwest the soil is usually referred to rather than the population. (See Unit XX.)

Dry farming: A technique of farming designed to take the utmost advantage of the scanty moisture available. Two elements are basic to dry farming: (1) planting in trenches between rows, and frequent plowing so that a mulch of dry soil hinders capillary action and evaporation; and (2) the breeding of strains which require less moisture than the older varieties of the same plant. It is this technique which has made cotton culture profitable in the western portions of Oklahoma and Texas where it has been developed to the point that, after relatively abundant rainfall in the winter, cotton may be harvested without the fall of any rain after it is planted.

It is suggested that the student read (or review) the assignment in *Human Geography of the South* very carefully, since it provides a more detailed discussion of the differences and the likenesses between the two portions of the South than was possible in *Southern Regions*. If a copy of *The Great Plains* is available, it also will be found very valuable in tracing the way in which the older culture of the regions east of the Mississippi was altered to meet new conditions found on the dry prairies. This author puts the situation dramatically by saying that in the older regions civilization rested on three legs—land, water, and timber—but that west of the 100th meridian two of these legs were withdrawn, and that consequently a new type of culture came into being.

D. Questions primarily on facts and mapograph interpretations

1. Compare the geographic factors in the Southeast with those in the Southwest, including rainfall, topography, temperature, etc. Indicate factors favorable to heavy machine (tractor, etc.) cotton farming.
2. Contrast methods of cotton farming in the Southeast with those in the Southwest. What factors enter into the differences noted?
3. Contrast size and population density of the two southern regions. What are some of the implications of these differences?
4. What are the principal urban centers of the Southwest? How do they differ from one another? How do they differ from the urban centers of the Southeast?
5. Compare the mineral wealth of the two southern regions. What are the principal differences and how do these differences affect the social situations in the two regions?
6. Compare the ports of the two regions as to tonnage handled and nature of products handled. Translate this comparison into terms of economic organization.
7. From the evidence of a railway map argue for or against the statement that the cultural currents of the Southwest flow inward. Check this conclusion against a map showing location of colleges or charts showing place of residence of college students within the region.
8. Compare the population composition of the two regions. What problems arise from the presence of distinct population groups?
9. What are the principal subregions of the Southwest? How do these subregions compare with those of the Southeast as to diversity?
10. From the map on page 186 it appears that the two subregions of the Southwest which are most distinctly urban are also prairie regions. Do you see any causal connection between these two facts?
11. How do you account for the fact that the last three states to be admitted to full political status are found within the Southwest? (Note an error at top of p. 181. Texas was admitted in 1845, not 1834.)
12. What explanation can you offer for the tables on page 180 showing that the two southern regions receive a higher percentage of relief funds than the population or internal revenue collections would entitle them to on a per capita

basis? Would this same explanation serve for similar situations in the Middle States?
13. How do you account for the numerous but small areas of specialized farming in the Southwest?
14. What is the connection between the newness of the Southwest and the difficulty in dividing the region into subregions? How does this difficulty appear on the map on page 186?

E. **Questions primarily on policy and program**
1. What effect on attitudes toward international relations would be expected from the fact that a high percentage of the Southwest's cotton enters export trade?
2. Northern Louisiana, northeastern Texas and southern Arkansas are contained in one huge petroleum producing district. What does this situation mean in terms of state governments? What means can you suggest for bettering existing conditions?
3. Taking into consideration the railway and waterway nets, and the non-material factors of tradition and the influence of existing trade relations, do you think the ports on the Gulf of Mexico will extend their spheres of influence further into the nation? If so, do you think those of one region will be more successful in this matter than those of the other? If so, those of which region?
4. What is the industrial outlook in the Southwest? How do the two regions compare in this respect at this time? What do you think will be the trend in the future? Why?
5. What explanation can you offer for the failure of the woolen industry to move into the Southwest as the cotton industry has moved into the Southeast? Do you think it would be good national policy to encourage such movement?
6. In much of the Southwest there are four distinct population groups—Anglo-Americans, Latin-Americans, American Indians, and Negro-Americans. Should this situation result in a richer or poorer culture? Why?
7. From your reading or from your general knowledge of the region, do you know of any remaining elements in the culture of the Southwest which are of Indian or Spanish origin? Why has this culture left such small traces?
8. What are the implications for regionalism in the abundance of petroleum in the Southwest? For sectionalism?
9. Of what value is the newness of the Southwest from the point of view of the regional planner?
10. From the point of view of the nation what is the best use which can be made of the "desert" country of the Southwest?

F. **Topics for debate and forum**
1. "Resolved: that the problems of the 'dust bowl' are of national importance."
2. Cities are of more importance to the Southwest than to the Southeast.

3. Discuss the relative importance of geographic and social factors in the Southeast and Southwest.
4. Debate the relative merits of per capita payment of internal revenue and proportion of population as bases for distribution of federal funds.
5. Discuss the advisability of setting freight rates at a point which would encourage the use of ports on the Gulf of Mexico rather than the Atlantic Ocean by states such as Missouri, Kansas, Nebraska, the Dakotas, Iowa, and Illinois.

NOTES

UNIT XXIV

TOWARDS REGIONAL PLANNING

Long, long ago it was said that "where there is no vision the people perish." It may be said of the southern people today that they have an encouraging number of leaders who can bend themselves to face facts, to analyze distressing conditions in their own land; who can then lift their minds and their eyes; who can take a hand in social reconstruction. Such leadership stands back of *Southern Regions*, its gathering and presenting of facts, the joint effort of many southern men and women. Such leadership plus good "followship," as the late E. C. Branson used to put it, are promises that better days are ahead and that to vision will be added the sort of planning so much needed in view of the facts. But good "followship" is dependent upon fact-facing, and here in summary are some of the things that must be reckoned with by the people, as seen by Donald Becker in *Plan Age* after he had studied the book, *Southern Regions:*

> Thus we have a picture of the Southeast as a land of paradox. Much natural wealth, yet social poverty. Region of farms, yet importer of foods and user of deficient diets. Potentially the garden spot of the earth, actually a region of broken hearts and backs. Abounding in traditions of good-living, actually lacking the means, oftentimes, of even a subsistence level of living. Traditions of humanism and Jeffersonian democracy juxtaposed to discouragement of the arts, religious intolerance, and racial prejudice. Highest ratio of human reproduction, yet losing the cream of its human wealth because unable to support it. Stronghold of Protestantism in the United States, leader in homicides and lynchings. Land of sunshine and open fields, land of undernourishment and tuberculosis. Technological deficiency, institutional inadequacy, human and physical waste, bigotry and demagoguery, above all else, *ignorance*—these epitomize the problem of regional planning in the Southeast.

Is it putting it too strong to affirm that the South, the Nation, even Civilization itself must either plan or perish? One thing is certain: the Southeast needs visionful, planful action that is not postponed too long. It is with this thought that the Southern Regional Study closes. The Southeast must somehow combine new motives and realisms with adequate steadiness and untiring action if the wide chasm between the region's possibilities and its actualities is to be bridged.

A. Aims for the student

1. To distinguish between realistic planning that faces facts intelligently and studiously, and the Utopianism, sentimentalism, and radicalism that is fed by loose theory, wishful thinking, and mere emotion.
2. To survey in summary the problems that the southern regions must grasp and master more vigorously with the assistance of the nation.
3. To propose a "hands-on" program of up-stream social engineering for southern reconstruction to take the place of a "hands-off" down-stream drift into more deficiency and stagnation.
4. To consider two 6-year plans that will set the pace for regional-national progress and show definite social reconstruction well on its way in the South and the nation by the year 1950.

B. Reading material for study

Southern Regions, Chapter I, pp. 187-205; Chapter XI. (Correction: in the first printing, page 195, the first word in the sixteenth line should be "charged.")

C. Definitions and general guidance

Utopia, Utopian: (Original Greek word meaning "not a place.") Impracticable schemes of social regeneration; the "Utopia" of Sir Thomas More (1478-1535) was an imaginary island of ideal human relationships. Utopian literature was quite prominent in earlier centuries when it was dangerous to denounce openly and straightforwardly the social ills of the time. Literary Utopias go back at least as far as Plato and Plutarch.

Socialization: Stated briefly this means an awareness of, and a desire to promote the rights, privileges, and responsibilities of others as well as oneself; what E. A. Ross means by "the development of the we-feeling in associates and their growth in capacity and will to act together."

Motivation: That which impels, moves, or drives an individual or group to action; to provide with a motive.

Transitional democracy or society: Transition has to do with the passage from one phase, condition, or stage to another. Constitutional amendments reflect transitional changes; recent political and economic transitions have lately marked international affairs; industrial transition in New England and agricultural transition in the South are now in process with transitional political accompaniments.

Differentials: Railroad rates, wages, etc., may vary from place to place. It has been customary, for example, to allow for a differential in living costs and wages in the South. (See top of p. 355.)

Research: Scientific investigation, classification, and presentation of facts.

TOWARDS REGIONAL PLANNING

D. and E. Questions on facts and policy

1. Can the Constitution of the United States be termed a social plan? Why or why not?
2. Can a bridge be built without basic theory that considers stresses and strains, direction and careful planning? Can societal difficulties be met and mastered by rule-of-thumb planlessness and drift?
3. Why is the public afraid of "planning"? What is the difference between "promiscuous experimentation" and controlled planning? Is there anything manifestly dangerous in the purposes of such an organization as the National Economic and Social Planning Association? Discuss; explain; give reasons.
4. Planning in the Southeast will require "rare strategy, skill, and boldness." Between pages 584 and 588 several aspects of culture are mentioned as needing these three attributes. Discuss them.
5. Why is planning for a "new diversity in both crops and types of farming" considered the key to regional reconstruction? What is the difference between soil exhaustion and soil erosion?
6. If cotton is doomed as a quantity cash crop for the Southeast, what sort of crop planning and planting will be necessary for Virginia, the Carolinas, Georgia, and Alabama? Is there any suggestion in the map on page 194 that the possible dairy crescent would be sufficient for the entire Southeast? What soil and health changes might be expected within a generation from such a dairy region and the utilization of its products?
7. In addition to the main problems mentioned as needing immediate adjustment (pp. 584-585), what others might be included?
8. If the South proposes to develop itself further without help from outside, how can it be done? So far, in what specific ways have certain funds assisted the South?
9. Does it seem that the South needs more research by and about itself, or does it need first to spread abroad the knowledge already in hand? Why?
10. Illustrate the three main approaches and the four basic requirements underlying these approaches discussed between pages 588 and 596.
11. Why are two 6-year periods of planning suggested rather than four 3-year periods or one 12-year period?

In connection with this last question: The first 6-year period, from 1937-1938 to 1943-1944, would allow for two or three state legislative sessions and for parts of three federal administrations. Such a period would be long enough for adequate legislation, but not too long. There would also be enough time for crop rotation, soil erosion service, rural rehabilitation and transfer of tenant farmers to a condition of land ownership; time enough for experimentation in livestock and seed breeding, in part-time industry and farming, in developing new industries, and in outlining new educational curricula and research programs; time enough also to train and apprentice workers for both old and new skills. The second 6-year period would be based on a priority schedule similar to the first; the differentiation between the two periods would be primarily to profit in the second by the experiences gained in the first.

Once more to combine our own views with those of *Plan Age:*

FUNDAMENTAL OBJECTIVES

1. Genuine liberalism that strives to maintain a quality civilization in a quantity world.
2. Democracy to be attained through redistribution of wealth by means of capacity to produce as well as more mature equalization and reintegration programs.
3. Increased wages, income, and values.
4. New quality in production.
5. More quantity-spread of the good things of life, both necessities and luxuries; expansion of the basic consumption capacity of the people especially in the Southeast.
6. A balanced agriculture for an increased value economy, in place of present emphasis on commercial farming.
7. New attitudes and tastes that mean the enrichment of life.

MAJOR STEPS IN ACHIEVING FUNDAMENTAL OBJECTIVES

1. Widespread recognition throughout the South and the nation of the seriousness of southern problems. (Read again paragraph 254 on page 187.) "Some aspects of this prospect are alarming. . . ." The people should know it.
2. General recognition that the problem of planning in the southeastern region is a national as well as a regional obligation.
3. Recognition of the need for gradualness in planning, adapting plans to a flexible democracy, and explaining plans to the people; even to children that they may grow up with the idea of direction rather than drift.
4. Comprehension by the South and by the nation of the size of the job.
5. A new awareness on the part of the nation of the logical evolution and growth of the Southeast's culture.
6. Nationally and regionally, ". . . the need for wiser counsel than the growing body of critics who tend to incite the South's marginal folk to violent revolution."
7. Recognition of the need for "a sort of moratorium on violent industrial and race conflict."
8. Understand the meaning of regionalism and replacing of the concept of sectionalism with that of regionalism.
9. Recognition of the limits of regional planning.

10. Coöperation instead of jealousies within and between the states of the region.
11. "Intelligent willingness to pay the price of progress. This means work, trained people, and patient persistence."
12. More realistic facing of facts.
13. Recognition of diminishing rôle of cotton in southeastern economy.
14. Increase of machine technology and the increased range of technology.
15. Recognition of the man-and-land importance of dairying in the agricultural reconstruction of the Southeast.
16. New diversity of crops and farming.
17. Restoration of soil; stop its exhaustion.
18. Protection of soil; attack upon erosion.
19. Recognition, in view of present man-land conditions, of the relative overcrowding of the Southeast with too many people returning to submarginal areas and homesteads.
20. More widespread recognition of the Negro as a special, but all-important aspect of regional planning in the Southeast.
21. Concentration of new educational institutions in a few key subregions.
22. Funds enough to permit proper launching, and to insure growth to maturity, of new educational institutions.
23. Revitalized education at all levels, especially for adults.
24. Recognition of importance of social experimentation.
25. Realization in the public and in the legislative mind that planning within two 6-year periods is possible, is needed, and should be functioning for southern reconstruction between the present and the middle of this twentieth century.

In a day when western waters are spanned by great highway-bridges—greater than the mind of man had dared to dream of in an earlier day and now a reality in the face of those who had said it "couldn't be done"—the time may be near when the region and the nation will build better social, economic, and political structures. But all great bridges require at least two major supports as well as countless properly fitted individual parts. Similarly, societal bridging of the chasm lying between actualities and possibilities calls for national and regional coöperation in which every citizen has a part. "Repeat again," says Dr. Odum, "the task is one not only for regional mastery but for national participation. It is a test of reintegration and equalization in the democratic process. . . . The urgency of the situation justifies the conclusion that this test of American Regionalism should be made before the turn of the mid-century." Will every citizen do his part?

The strength of a democracy depends finally upon the people themselves, their ability to see, to study, and to move realistically in the direction of life, liberty, and happiness.

BOOK LIST FOR FURTHER READING

Cauley, T. J. *Agrarianism.* 1935.*
Chase, Stuart. *Rich Land, Poor Land.* New York, McGraw-Hill, 1936.
Couch, W. T., ed. *Culture in the South.* 1934.*
Dabney, Virginius. *Liberalism in the South.* 1932.*
Johnson, C. S., Embree, E. R., and Alexander, W. W. *The Collapse of Cotton Tenancy.* 1935.*
Johnson, Gerald. *The Wasted Land.* 1937.*
Mims, Edwin. *The Advancing South.* Garden City, Doubleday, Page & Co., 1926.
Odum, H. W. *An American Epoch; Southern Portraiture in the National Picture.* New York, Holt, 1930.
Raper, A. F. *Preface to Peasantry.* 1936.*
Twelve Southerners. *I'll Take My Stand.* New York, Harper, 1930.
Vance, R. B. *Human Geography of the South.* 1932.*
Zimmermann, E. W. *World Resources and Industries.* New York, Harper, 1933.

* Published by the University of North Carolina Press, Chapel Hill, North Carolina.

INDEX OF DEFINITIONS

ABUNDANCE potentialities, 37
Actualities, deficiency, 37
Adult education, 108
Age of consent, 130
Agrarian culture, 52
Agrarianism, 82
Agricultural-industrial equilibrium, 163
Artificial wealth, 44
Assimilation, 100
Assumptions, unthinking mass, 27

BLACK Belt: people, 153; soil, 153, 179

CAPITAL wealth, 44
Cash crop, 82
Chemurgic, 68
Chemurgy, 164
Chronological lag, 171
Chronological strata, 146
Colonial economy, 82
Composite products, 37
Consent, age of, 130
Conservatives, 36
Coöperative purchasing, 68
Coöperative selling, 68
Cross fertilization, 163
Cultural pathology, 12
Culture, 10; agrarian, 52
Culture complex, 45
Culture (cultural) inbreeding, 29
Culture (cultural) lag, 29
Cumulative emergency, 38
Cumulative handicaps, 37

DECENTRALIZATION, 88
Deficiency, submarginal, 38
Deficiency actualities, 37
Delinquency, 130
Demagogue, political, 123
Democracy, transitional, 186
Demography, 11, 52
Denominator, regional, 36
Dichotomous, 28
Dichotomy, 28
Differentials, 186
Diffusion, racial, 100
Distributive occupations, 147
Dominance of characteristics, 20
Dry farming, 179
Dynamics, 20

ECONOMIC nerves, 179
Economy, colonial, 82; money, 45; value, 45
Education, adult, 108; liberal, 108; vocational, 108
Educational equalization, 108
Entity, socio-economic, 154
Equalization, educational, 108

Equilibration, 45
Equilibrium, 45; agricultural-industrial, 163
Ethnic, 100
Excise tax, 124
Experiment, national-regional, 163
Extension service, 108
Extension work, 108
Extractive occupations, 147

FOLK, marginal, 153
Folk-regional society, 11
Folkways, 46
Foreign-born, 100
Framework, 10
Functional analysis, 12

HETEROGENEITY, 153
Homogeneity, 153
Human wealth, 44

IDEALISM, 12
Ideology, 131
Imaginative exploration, 61. *See also* Romantic realism
Immaturity, 12
Inbreeding, cultural, 29
Incidence, 28
Income, 76
Income tax, 123
Index number, 123
Industry, decentralization of, 88
Institutional services, 45
Institutions, 146
Inter-regional optima, 38

LAG, 82; chronological, 171; culture (cultural), 29; time, 138
Laissez faire, 100
Land, marginal, 153
Land-grant college, 108
Leadership, national, 123
Legume, 68
Liberal education, 108
Liberals, 36

MARGINAL folk, 153
Marginal land, 153
Marginal subsistence, 37, 153
Marginality, 12, 37, 153
Median, 13
Metropolitan district, 100
Minority group, 100
Mobility, 82
Money-economy, 45
Mores, 60
Mothers' aid, 131
Motivation, 186
Multiple subregions, 12

NATIONAL Conference of Social Work, 131
National leadership, 123
National-regional experiment, 163
Native-born, 100
Native white, 100
Natural resources, 60
Natural wealth, 44
Naval stores, 88
Non-liquidity, 44
Norm, 38

OBJECTIVE measures, 37
Occupations: extractive, 147; distributive, 147; social, 147
One-crop system, 68
Optima, inter-regional, 38
Optimum realization, 61
Optimum setting, 20

PARDON, 131
Parole, 131
Pathology, cultural, 12
Patterns, 28
Political demagogue, 123
Poll tax, 123
Potentialities, abundance, 37
Priority schedules, 13
Private social service, 131
Public social service, 131
Public welfare, 131

QUALITY characteristics, 28
Quartile, 13

RACIAL diffusion, 100
Radicals, 36
Rationalization, 11
Reactionaries, 36
Realism, 12; romantic, 45
Regimen, 38
Regional denominator, 36
Regionalism, 11, 163
Rehabilitation, vocational, 131
Reintegration, 38
Religion, 138
Research, 186

Romantic realism, 45. *See also* Imaginative exploration

SALES tax, 123
Science, 138
Sectionalism, 11, 163
Severance tax, 124
Socialization, 186
Social occupations, 147
Social service, 131
Social work, 131
Societal behavior, 100
Societal evolution, 29
Socio-economic entity, 154
State portraiture, 171
Stateways, 46
Stereotype, 147
Strata, chronological, 146
Submarginal deficiency, 38
Subregions, multiple, 12
Superabundance, 61

TANGIBLE wealth, 76
Tax, 123; excise, 124; income, 123; poll, 123; sales, 123; severance, 124
Taxation, 123
Technique, 20
Technological, 88
Technology, 88
Tenancy, 82
Time-lag, 138
Time quality, 12
Transitional democracy, 186

URBANIZATION, 88
Utopia, 186
Utopian, 186

VALUE-ECONOMY, 45
Vocational education, 108
Vocational rehabilitation, 131

WAGE differential, 100, 186
Wages, 76
Wealth, artificial, 44; capital, 44; human, 44; natural, 44; tangible, 76
Welfare, public, 131
Workable techniques, 20

www.ingramcontent.com/pod-product-compliance
Lightning Source LLC
Chambersburg PA
CBHW080410300426
44113CB00015B/2466